Political Ecology

Political Ecology
System Change
Not Climate Change

Dimitrios Roussopoulos

Revised and expanded

Montréal/Chicago/London

Copyright © 2019 Black Rose Books

Thank you for purchasing this Black Rose Books publication. No part of this book may be reproduced or transmitted in any form, by any means electronic or mechanical including photocopying and recording, or by any information storage or retrieval system—without written permission from the publisher, or, in the case of photocopying or other reprographic copying, a license from the Canadian Copyright Licensing Agency, Access Copyright, with the exception of brief passages quoted by a reviewer in a newspaper or magazine. If you acquired an illicit electronic copy of this book, please consider making a donation to Black Rose Books.

Black Rose Books No. T503

Library and Archives Canada Cataloguing in Publication

Title: Political ecology : system change not climate change / Dimitri Roussopoulos.
Names: Roussopoulos, Dimitrios I., author.
Description: 4th edition, revised. | Previous edition had subtitle: The climate crisis and a new social agenda.
Identifiers: Canadiana (print) 20189017570 | Canadiana (ebook) 20189017589 | ISBN 9781551646534 (hardcover) | ISBN 9781551646510 (softcover) | ISBN 9781551646558 (PDF)
Subjects: LCSH: Human ecology—Political aspects. | LCSH: Environmental protection—Citizen participation. | LCSH: Environmental policy. | LCSH: Green movement.
Classification: LCC JA75.8 .R68 2019 | DDC 363.7/05613—dc23

C.P.35788 Succ. Léo-Pariseau
Montréal, QC, H2X 0A4
Canada
Explore our books and subscribe to our newsletter:
www.blackrosebooks.com

Ordering Information

USA/INTERNATIONAL	CANADA	UK/IRELAND
University of Chicago Press Chicago Distribution Center 11030 South Langley Avenue Chicago IL 60628	University of Toronto Press 5201 Dufferin Street Toronto, ON M3H 5T8	Central Books 50 Freshwater Road Chadwell Heath, London RM8 1RX
(800) 621-2736 (USA) (773) 702-7000 (International) orders@press.uchicago.edu	1-800-565-9523 utpbooks@utpress.utoronto.ca	+44 (0) 20 8525 8800 contactus@centralbooks.com

Black Rose Books is a not-for-profit publishing project of Cercle Noir et Rouge

CONTENTS

PREFACE 2019   7

PREFACE   31

ONE   37
    The State Management of the Environment

TWO   71
    Citizens' Responses to the Plight of the Earth

THREE   97
    Political Ecology and Social Ecology

FOUR   123
    A Road Map Beyond Mere Environmentalism

FIVE   141
    The New Politics of Social Ecology

EPILOGUES   151

POSTSCRIPT   156
    After Paris COP21 – What Next?

NOTES   187

Acknowledgements: This book benefited greatly from the editorial work of my friend and colleague Andrea Levy. I would also like to thank Linda Barton, for her work on one of the sections of the book, and April Hubert, for her help with the word processing and layout of the first edition.

The revised edition of this book would have been impossible without the attentive devotion and editorial oversight of Nathan McDonnell. My appreciation is expressed to both Nathan and also Eirik Eiglad of New Compass in Oslo. These two dear comrades reflect a new generation that is helping in the transformation of our society.

PREFACE

2019

"On a foreign visit today to California, the USA Leader (he wore a USA cap so the Californians would know where he's from) declared that had the people of California done 'more raking these fires wouldn't happen.' He repeated that there is no 'climate change' but 'I want great climate.'"

> —Documentary filmmaker Michael Moore's tweet following US President Donald Trump's visit to California in the wake of the unprecedented 2018 fires.

The first half of Donald Trump's presidency has redefined our understanding of "outrageous." The rollercoaster of bombast and absurdity—the constant stream of headlines about the lies, scandals, corruption, and treason—can easily distract us from, even numb us to, the ruthlessness of Trump's agenda.

With a leather folder and a pen, seated at a mahogany table surrounded by a cabal of domineering plutocrats, military generals, and crypto-fascists, Trump has led a wholesale assault on marginalized groups and liberal social policies. He has signed the most executive orders of any president in half a century,[1] making his time in office an extreme experiment in right-wing social engineering.

We should not kid ourselves: the climate catastrophe is an epic war of the rich on the poor; corporate criminality on a global scale. Just one hundred corporations are responsible for 71% of emissions,[2] but it is the world's poor who will overwhelmingly suffer. With billions of dollars at their disposal, these corporations have for decades been sabotaging environmental action, buying off politicians, and funding climate denialism. This assault is not new; it's the continuation of an old political project, though it has never been so naked as today.

Trump's War on the Earth and our Health

President Trump's all-out war on the environment began with his appointment of former senator and Attorney General of Oklahoma, Scott Pruitt, as Administrator of the Environmental Protection Agency (EPA). As a climate denier who received substantial campaign contributions from the fossil fuel industry and even sued the EPA at least 14 times on behalf of polluting industries, Pruitt was the last person one would have wanted to run the agency. After seventeen months in the job, and while facing 14 separate federal investigations into his spending habits, conflicts of interest, extreme secrecy, and management practices, he then resigned, only to be replaced by former coal lobbyist Andrew Wheeler. Ironic appointments to key agencies are a running theme of Trump's presidency. Three of Trump's transition team, who were supposed to guide his Native American policies, have been funded by the Koch brothers—the owners of the second largest privately owned company in the US, Koch Industries, which specializes in the oil, chemical, and mining industries.

The administration has enthusiastically served the interests of industry—especially the coal, petroleum, fracking, and uranium industries—to the detriment of the environment and human health. Arguing that regulations see "billions of dollars drained from our economy," Trump's presidency has been busy reversing more than 70 environmental rules (as of July 2018), either by presidential executive order without informing the public or by the EPA under Pruitt or Wheeler. A Harvard University report found that these changes alone would lead to a staggering 80,000 additional deaths each decade in the US, with even more deaths internationally. Trump declared without irony: "We are going to get rid of the regulations that are just destroying us. You can't breathe—you cannot breathe."[3]

The sweeping changes have included:

- the announced withdrawal of the US from the Paris Accord on global warming
- a cut in contributions to the international Green Climate Fund
- the crippling of renewable energy research

- the announced repeal of the Clean Power Plan (this alone is expected to cause an estimated 36,000 US deaths and 630,000 cases of respiratory ailments in American children)
- the aggressive roll-back of Obama-era restrictions on air pollution, including those related to ozone, methane emissions, and the toxic emissions of the fossil fuels industry and industrial manufacturers
- the removal of restrictions on acceptable levels of coal-ash waste, the release of pollutants, and the dumping of mining waste into public waterways
- the repeal of regulations on the construction, pollution, and clean-up of oil rigs and mines
- the opening of nearly all of America's coastal waters (including the Arctic) to offshore oil and gas drilling
- the opening of public and Native American lands (including national monument land and land in or near national parks) to mining, including fracking
- approval of the fiercely contested Keystone XL and Dakota Access pipelines
- overturning protections for endangered species and restrictions on hunting and commercial fishing
- suspension of the Clean Water Rule (which protects waterways for a third of the population)
- weakening of restrictions on hydrofluorocarbons, pesticides, toxic chemicals, and lead paint
- removal of the mandate that proposed federal infrastructure projects should take into account flood standards, impact on climate change, and local environmental impact
- limitations on the authority of government to conduct environmental review processes, do environmental

planning, and use health data to make environmental policy.[4]

As the Obama-era environmental reforms—sheepishly modest as they were—are being flushed down the toilet, it is difficult to avoid the sinking feeling that our collective destiny is under grave attack and we are powerless to stop it.

***

How did we get into this mess? The standard interpretation of the 2016 election is that Trump was voted in by frustrated white working-class men from post-industrial wastelands; they were angry at the world and clawed for redemption through chauvinistic populism. The whole psychosocial dynamic that many believe led to Trump's election was actually foreseen two decades ago, with eerie prescience, by the American philosopher Richard Rorty:

> Something will crack.... The nonsuburban electorate will decide that the system has failed and start looking around for a strongman to vote for—someone willing to assure them that, once he is elected, the smug bureaucrats, tricky lawyers, overpaid bond salesmen, and postmodernist professors will no longer be calling the shots....
>
> One thing that is very likely to happen is that the gains made in the past 40 years by black and brown Americans, and by homosexuals, will be wiped out. Jocular contempt for women will come back into fashion.... All the resentment which badly

> educated Americans feel about having their manners dictated
> to them by college graduates will find an outlet.[5]

Cathartic for the days following Trump's election, this passage went viral.

The election was decades in the making. Decades of a corporate *coup d'état* with the collaboration of politicians chanting the Thatcherist mantra "there is no alternative." Decades of technocratic rule that only became more contemptuous of the needs of the poor and working classes. Decades of the ossification of the media into servile lap dogs and smug cynics. Decades of the Left's betrayal of working class struggles as it retreated into monastic cultural theory and a phony facade of progressivism.

The ecstatic scream of Trump's supporters was really a panicked fury. Resentful at the elitist ruling classes, and bitterly afraid of losing their place in a neoliberal world, a class in existential crisis mounted a vengeful revolt. But rather than striking at the stratified and exploitative capitalist system itself, this understandable class rage has fuelled a reactionary revival of old hatreds towards easy victims. And for people who felt under siege by Muslims, gender neutral bathrooms, and Chinese exports, Trump emerged as a "saviour".

Trump has channelled the alienation of the (largely white) working classes and underclasses by denouncing the corrupt US political system and the "deep state," represented by establishment politicians on both sides. But he wasn't just speaking to fringe conspiracy theorists. He tapped into currents of distrust widely held in the US. Between 50% and 75% of US citizens believe that unelected military, intelligence, and government officials secretly manipulate or direct national policy, according to polls.[6] Why does it take a bullying billionaire to call out the system for what it is? Where was the voice of the Left?

The Democratic Party will not Save Us

> The best lack all conviction, while the worst
> Are full of passionate intensity.
>
> —*The Second Coming*, by W. B. Yeats (1919)

During the worst of successive Republican government excesses, righteous howls can be heard from the other side of the aisle. We could be forgiven for imagining the Democrats as the "good guys" rescuing us from the Republican nasties: that as long as we vote them in they will fix the mess and steer the nation to safety. But the Democrats' attempts to capitalize on Republican blunders is pure hypocrisy. At best, the Democrats offer only symbolism, mere tinkering at the edges of a corrupt system. At worst, they are a morally bankrupt mirror image of what the Republicans used to be.

Trump cut the Democrats' lunch, stealing much of the base that the Democratic National Congress (DNC) had for so long betrayed. He was able to credibly brand Clinton as a Wall Street puppet. Apart from Clinton's infamous $675,000 private speeches to Goldman Sachs, high finance's grip on the Democrats is evident in its campaign donations. Clinton had twice as many six-figure donors as Trump. The same was true of the "hope-and-dreams" president Obama. Wall St donated 50% more to Obama than to John McCain in the

2008 campaign.[7] Immediately following the 2008 election, in a huge corporate heist, the Obama administration bailed out the parasitic banks who were criminally responsible for the Global Financial Crisis. Yet the poor were abandoned to an epidemic of foreclosures and unemployment.

Trump also railed against free trade agreements for sending jobs to China. One of his first reforms was to rip up the Trans-Pacific Partnership (TPP), a 5,600-page agreement, secretly negotiated, that empowers multinationals at the cost of state sovereignty, labor rights, and the environment. On the other hand, it was Obama who curiously championed the TPP in his final year in office, criss-crossing the Pacific to promote it.

Trump also criticized how establishment foreign policy led to entanglement in endless foreign wars. In Napoleonic fashion, Clinton symbolized *par excellence* the liberal face of aggressive US imperialism. During her term as Secretary of State, the US escalated drone warfare in the Middle East; militarily intervened (directly or indirectly) in Afghanistan, Iraq, Syria, Pakistan, Yemen, Mali, Libya, and Somalia; dangerously sabre-rattled with Russia and China; pursued heroic whistleblowers like Julian Assange of Wikileaks, Chelsea Manning, and Edward Snowden; and overturned democratically elected governments like that of Honduras.

People are tired of the Democratic party's Janus-faced hypocrisy and centrist moral bankruptcy. And rightly so. People are uninspired by the neoliberal centrism of the Democratic Party, which only benefits those in the party who are cosy with big business. Audacity is what inspires people, not mediocre accommodationism.[8] Meanwhile, the cultural politics of diversity and political correctness are used to paper over the Democratic Party's support for neoliberalism and militarism. More geneneally, when the Left abandons working class struggles for a condescending smugness and slick careerism, there should be no surprise that the counterattack of the Right is so focused on a "commonsense" critique of politically correct cultural and identity politics.

For so long, the system has been waging war on us. It is about time we fought back. And, no, voting for the Democratic Party is not the solution. We need to lose all illusions they will come to the rescue. That the system can be reformed with better people or laws. Or that electoralism generally is the way for things to change. We need to go further.

What about Bernie Sanders and the openly socialist youthful movement he helped inspire? Although it was promising that his campaign voiced a critique of capitalism and extreme inequality, it hasn't translated into a movement that is truly challenging the power structure. Why? Because it hasn't tried to: it's not about building the force of a grassroots people-power movement that can really confront the powers-that-be.

This shows the contradictions of being locked into an electoralist strategy inside representative democracy and the limitations of a reformist logic tinkering with the symptoms of capitalism. It is largely about mobilizing for elections once every four years to get "good" candidates into office, not about building an ongoing force of grassroots opposition outside of Congress or parliaments. It is about lining up behind charismatic politicians (like Sanders), a popularity contest which reinforces egotistical careerism and even creates personality cults. This is counter to a spirit of grassroots-led direct democracy, of ordinary people collectively deciding their destiny on a daily basis.[9]

If Trump and the Tea Party can mobilize people with a fundamentalist zeal and try to aggressively reengineer society for corporate feudalism, why can't the Left be just as audacious? Why can't we proudly and unflinchingly call for a fully egalitarian and ecological society? Have we forgotten the urgency of the classic anticapitalist imperative of "socialism or barbarism?" (Or, as reformulated by Bookchin for the late 20th century, "ecology or catastrophe!") American literary critic and political theorist Frederic Jameson ironically charged that, with the dominance of "capitalist realism," as he called it, "It is easier to imagine the end of the world than the end of capitalism."

We don't have time to lazily indulge in fantasies about the end of the world. Nor to defend high-brow politically-correct middle class liberalism—a morally bankrupt reformism that so easily deludes us into a complacent coma. Let us instead get to building radical social movements that totally re-envision society and our relationship with nature. Now is the time for a social revolution. And, now, there really is no alternative.

Deadlock at the 2018 Midterms

The storm clouds are moving in, and the warnings of scientists are becoming ever more dire. A month before the US midterm elections, the Intergovernmental Panel on Climate Change (IPCC) released a new assessment prepared by 99 climate scientists, citing 6,000 sources, that warns that we have 12 years to prevent runaway climate change. The report claims that "rapid, far-reaching, and unprecedented changes in all aspects of society by 2030" would be necessary to limit warming to 1.5 degrees Celsius, which would be far less catastrophic than 2 degrees Celsius.[10] A month later, the US government published its own report produced by top climate scientists and coordinated by six government agencies that predicts local impacts on the US, foreseeing effects such as a greater risk of wildfires in California, coastal flooding in the Southeastern states, drought for Midwest farmers, and extreme heat in the Southern Great Plains.[11] A week later, another international report warned that 2018 was set to the be the fourth warmest year on record; 2015–18 were already the four warmest.[12]

Not that we need more statistics or reports to convince us of the urgency of the situation. What's clear is that the level of effort we need is to mobilize entire economies around climate change as if it was a wartime existential threat.

Many had hoped that public outrage after two years of a Trump presidency would translate into a tidal wave against the Republicans in the US midterms. But US electoral politics is as divided as ever, and the Democrats were not able to captivate the public with an inspiring vision for society. The elections resulted in a political deadlock as the Democrats gained control of the House and the Republicans continued to control the Senate. The environmental crisis was but a minor concern, demonstrating that, despite imminent danger, it is not yet recognized as a serious issue in US politics.

There were, to be sure, some notable ballot initiatives. Floridians banned offshore oil drilling. In Nevada and

Arizona, where the sun shines more than 200 days a year, ballot measures would have forced utility corporations to capture more solar power and ditch fossil fuels faster than currently planned. But only Nevada supported this measure; it was rejected in Arizona. One of the causes of falling solar costs is investment from 29 states, led by California, that have already committed to renewable energy mandates. In California, an attempt to repeal the gas tax failed, which is good news for the ambitious public transit projects it will subsidize. In some places, attempts to draw attention to climate action faltered and utility companies and other fossil fuel advocates won the day. Washington State voters narrowly rejected a ballot question that would have established the nation's first carbon fee. The closely-watched showdown was lost with 56 percent against—the second time such an initiative was defeated. In Colorado, the fossil fuel industry spent $40 million to successfully fend off an attempt to impose a half-mile buffer between drilling operations and people's homes.[13]

The midterms saw some inspirational activism by young people. One example was The Sunrise Movement, a youth-led grassroots climate justice group combining advocacy, electoral campaigning, and direct action to push for a Green New Deal. At the time of writing in December 2018, their proposals have galvanized support from several left-wing Democrats newly elected to Congress. They even occupied the offices of Democratic House Leader Nancy Pelosi, with freshly-elected Alexandria Ocasio-Cortez, the youngest woman ever to serve in Congress, delivering a speech to the young activists during the occupation.[14] Ocasio-Cortez herself has emphasized that we need a wartime organization of social and economic capital in order for a Green New Deal to succeed.

We Need to Name the System

Electoralist reformism barely scratches the surface. We must address the system at its roots. This book proposes deep systemic change through a democratic grassroots revolution. We can transform this destructive, exploitative economic and political machine into an egalitarian, ecological, and profoundly democratic society.

First, let us differentiate "environmentalists" and ecologists. The former merely manage destruction. They tweak policy and technology to attempt to lessen pollution, but leave a rotten system untouched. Ecologists, however, demand the system be cut at its roots. They condemn the eternal quest for "economic growth"—the cause of both disastrous inequality and the war on nature. The solution requires that we transform our relationships with each other as much as our relationships with nature. This is a more realistic roadmap, one that will require patient, long-term building.

We must start by naming the system—being willing to use the "C word": Capitalism. The first major anti-Vietnam War demonstration, 25,000 people strong, was organized by the Students for a Democratic Society (SDS) in Washington DC in 1965. On that day, SDS president Paul Potter delivered an activist homily that inspired the group to take a more radical approach to US foreign policy. His exhortation became known as the 'Naming the System' speech:

What kind of system is it that justifies the United States or any country seizing the destinies of the Vietnamese people and using them callously for its own purpose? What kind of system is it that disenfranchizes people in the South, leaves millions upon millions of people throughout the country impoverished and excluded from the mainstream and promise of American society, that creates faceless and terrible bureaucracies and makes those the place where people spend their lives and do their work...

We must name that system. We must name it, describe it, analyze it, understand it and change it. For it is only when that system is changed and brought under control that there can be any hope for stopping the forces that create a war in Vietnam today or a murder in the South tomorrow or all the incalculable, innumerable more subtle atrocities that are worked on people all over—all the time.[15]

Potter put his finger on the culprit—capitalism and imperialism—and recognized the need for a massive social movement with a radical vision to transform the system. Although millions of idealistic individuals struggle against the problem by trying to improve their personal consumption—changing light bulbs, driving less, recycling, and the rest—clearly the key culprits are the massive corporations that currently run our economy, our politics, our media. But how can we push for genuine change when they have so much power?

We Need to Block the Machine

Is it enough to politely ask for change, hoping we'll convince the politicians by the force of our argument? How has that worked out for us so far, while massive corporations heavily invested in industries such as fossil fuels still have their way in the halls of power and on the airwaves? Or will we force change through sheer defiance, drawing a line in the sand which cannot be ignored? To shake up the status quo, we'll need far more audacious actions: mass civil disobedience, including marches, sit-ins, blockades, and strikes. We need to block the system. Although we may sometimes feel powerless in this enormous corporate-run circus, they are counting on our apathetic complicity, our passive submission. They need it. So we need to deny it to them.

In 1961, an important split occurred in the anti-nuclear movement in Britain. Just as its leading organization in Britain, the Campaign for Nuclear Disarmament (CND), was becoming better known by the media, the philosopher, mathematician, and social activist Bertrand Russell quit as its first president. With a hundred supporters and a large meeting in London, he created a new campaign of mass civil disobedience. The movement took the name of The Committee of 100. Russell explained his reasoning in an article in *The New Statesman*:

> There is a very widespread feeling that however bad [government] policies may be, there is nothing that private people can do about it. This is a complete mistake. If all those who disapprove of government policy were to join massive

demonstrations of civil disobedience, they could render government wholly impossible and compel the so-called statesmen to acquiesce in measures that would make human survival possible. Such a vast movement, inspired by outraged public opinion, is possible, perhaps it is imminent. If you join it you will be doing something important to preserve your family, compatriots and the world.[16]

We must refuse to tolerate a corrupt system. Even if it involves "putting our bodies on the gears." Such was the cry of Mario Savio, a student leader of the 1960s Free Speech Movement at Berkeley, in a speech become legendary:

There is a time when the operation of the machine becomes so odious, makes you so sick at heart, that you can't take part. You can't even passively take part! And you've got to put your bodies upon the gears and upon the wheels, upon the levers, upon all the apparatus, and you've got to make it stop! And you've got to indicate to the people who run it, to the people who own it—that unless you're free, the machine will be prevented from working at all![17]

Why break the law? Why not try a more collaborative process of discussion and negotiation? Martin Luther King Jr. responds in a letter from a jail in Birmingham, Alabama:

You may well ask: "Why direct action? Why sit-ins, marches and so forth? Isn't negotiation a better path?" You are quite right in calling for negotiation. Indeed, this is the very purpose of direct action. Nonviolent direct action seeks to create such a crisis and foster such a tension that a community which has constantly refused to negotiate is forced to confront the issue. It seeks so to dramatize the issue that it can no longer be ignored. My citing the creation of tension as part of the work of the nonviolent resister may sound rather shocking. But I must confess that I am not afraid of the word "tension."[18]

Non-violent direct action is an integral part of a broader grassroots movement for social change that has a positive vision and clear proposals. When the "powers-that-be" refuse you a seat at the table, it's time to flip that table over. Our social movements must step up to the task. We've already proven our mettle. The "Battle for Seattle" in 1999 shut down the World Trade Organization (WTO) meeting despite the declaration of martial law. "Mission accomplished." At the 2001 Summit of the Americas, we shut down Quebec City and sent a proposed "Free Trade Area of the Americas" into the dustbin of history. Another exemplary victory. And even though the results of the Arab Spring have been mixed, it showed that people power is enough to overthrow regimes across entire regions.

In the climate movement, the next chapter is already rolling out around the world. For example, a new social movement called Extinction Rebellion coordinated days of nonviolent direct action in the centre of London in November 2018 that resulted in 82 arrests, and shut down several bridges during peak hour, with a people's assembly and blockade outside the Houses of Parliament. Several individuals even glued themselves to the gates of Downing Street and Buckingham Palace. Ordinary people, young and old, with flags and smiles, put their bodies in the way of the system and remained cheerful as police carried them off for arrest.

This same resistance was featured in the epic struggle against the Keystone XL pipeline. Civil disobedience often brought construction to a standstill, buying time for more permanent victories. The resistance wasn't just young white protestors. It was an alliance of local farmers, ecological activists, and indigenous peoples all along the proposed route of the pipeline and in the nation's capital, engaging in countless protests, blockades, direct actions, and tree climbs, in tandem with court cases. This battle is far from over.

Then there was Standing Rock, the spark for an inspiring renaissance in grassroots indigenous activism across the USA and Canada. At the historic 2017 indigenous-led protests, in North Dakota, thousands of people, indigenous and their allies, gathered together in a ten month camp to blockade the Dakota Access Pipeline. These protestors embodied values of decolonization, non-violence, and egalitarian community living as they stared down terrifyingly militarized police, National Guard, and mercenary forces. The activists' courage and passion captured the imagination of movements in the US and around the world; the action soon found support in an international divestment campaign targeting financial links with the pipeline. Although the blockade was brutally crushed following the election of Trump, this spirit of indigenous-led resistance to fossil fuel projects mushroomed throughout the US. The story is recounted in the powerful 2017 documentary *Awake, A Dream From Standing Rock*.

Protest and civil disobedience are vital, but alone they are not enough. Our movements must look beyond winning merely piecemeal reforms. They must present an inspiring vision for a different society. We need to, in the words of social ecologist Murray Bookchin: "Democratize the republic, and radicalize the democracy."

We Need A New Politics

Bringing the current "powers-that-be" to the table, and then to heel, will require immense action. Economic actions include strikes, boycotts, and creating an alternative economy while civil disobedience could include trespass, sit-ins, and occupations. Eventually, the tipping point will be passed, with actions against all central power: from conscientious objection and mutiny, to constructive revenue diversion. Recall the movement for conscientious objection to military taxation and Mahatma Gandhi's movement to boycott British goods.

Most importantly, we must establish a parallel government consisting in a direct democracy to create a situation of dual power. Top-down undemocratic corporate capitalism based on profit and authoritarianism would be challenged by the existence of a bottom-up, democratic, decentralized system based on respect, ecology, and community need. This democratic innovation would function as a counterpower to the State, rivalling and then eventually replacing it.

One of the greatest assets in our struggle is our cities. They are an enormous source of economic, legal, and institutional power and the closest level of government to the people. It is notable that the ancient Greek word for city is "*polis*," which also denotes a body of citizens and is the root of the English word "politics." Cities have always been the seats of economic power and civilization and, today, are the centre of resistance.

We must create a network of democratic, ecological city governments and reorganize regional economies. How? We should decentralize power to neighbourhood citizen assemblies—direct democracy will ensure decisions are made at human scale. We should democratize the economy: businesses should become cooperatives and communes, so that workers, consumers, and the wider community make the decisions about production and distribution. Communities and municipalities could prevent gentrification and speculation by taking over the ownership of the land, allowing them to provide for housing as a human right.[19] Neighbourhood assemblies would be federated across a city, producing a network of government by the people; cities would be federated even to a global scale to coordinate international relations. Power and wealth should be in the hands of the people and not corporations, politicians, or bureaucracies.

Then, we can redesign civilization based on ecological intelligence and need over greed. Polluting mega-industries will be supplanted by more sensible human-scale production. Mindless urbanization would be swept away in favour of more creative planning of urban and rural spaces—for the next hundreds of years and not just a few economic cycles. We will need to do the patient work of community organising and popular education so that community democracy can grow from the roots up.

Major thinkers like Murray Bookchin, Jane Jacobs, and Benjamin Barber foresaw such a movement. Barber noted recently that cities are already marshalling institutional power, resources, and law to confront national power with urban power. Trump is one of their targets. US cities produce half the nation's GDP. The world's cities combined produce 80% of GDP. A preponderance of taxes come from cities. Their power is enormous. And people power, when concentrated, is formidable.

Just one of the radical proposals by urbanists is to withhold taxes from central government. Barber explained this logic:

> 'We (cities) produce the wealth. You are not going to give it back to us; we'll keep it. Come and get it.' That's a revolutionary act.[20]

The C40 Cities, an alliance of urban centres doing something about climate change, produced many similar ideas at the 2018 Global Climate Action Summit in San Francisco. Cities must do more than just complain and resist. They must declare that:

> We have the democratic majority. We are the source of wealth creation. We are the source of universities. We are the source of culture. And we will not be bullied by a minority that has taken over the federal government and is trying to impose on the cities by encroaching on the rights of citizens, the rights of immigrants, and the rights of minorities.[21]

Every worthwhile left-inspired project—whether it's the minimum wage, the defence of human rights, humane immigration policy, or climate action—is now an urban movement, a local blooming of grassroots action. Cities have always been more conducive to making power accountable to the people. They have from the beginning facilitated inclusion, mobility, outreach, and trade. To be cosmopolitan is to reach out to one's neighbour—whether across the street or whole regions. From the 13th century to the 15th century, the Hanseatic League of German Cities made mutual agreements to overcome the domination of the ruling principalities. In the 1500s, the League of Mediterranean Cities stood throughout that region against imperial borders and ancient principalities. What will the cities of the new millennium bring to the table?

Around the world, national governments are becoming more reactionary and parochial, even while cities are more cosmopolitan. This gives cities a key role in building dual power or parallel government. Needless to say, for cities to assume this mantle they must become *more* democratic and ecological, and they must confederate with each other.[22]

This is what this book is about, with a roadmap that is realistic. In conclusion, 15-year-old activist Greta Thurnberg sums it up best in her speech at the 24th Conference of the Parties to the United Nations Framework Convention on Climate Change (COP24):

> My name is Greta Thunberg. I am 15 years old. I am from Sweden. I speak on behalf of Climate Justice Now. Many people say that Sweden is just a small country and it doesn't matter what we do. But I've learned you are never too small to make a difference. And if a few children can get headlines all over the world just by not going to school, then imagine what we could all do together if we really wanted to.

Preface to the 2019 edition

But to do that, we have to speak clearly, no matter how uncomfortable that may be. You only speak of green eternal economic growth because you are too scared of being unpopular. You only talk about moving forward with the same bad ideas that got us into this mess, even when the only sensible thing to do is [to] pull the emergency brake. You are not mature enough to tell it like is. Even that burden you leave to us children. But I don't care about being popular. I care about climate justice and the living planet. Our civilization is being sacrificed for the opportunity of a very small number of people to continue making enormous amounts of money. Our biosphere is being sacrificed so that rich people in countries like mine can live in luxury. It is the sufferings of the many which pay for the luxuries of the few.

The year 2078, I will celebrate my 75th birthday. If I have children maybe they will spend that day with me. Maybe they will ask me about you. Maybe they will ask why you didn't do anything while there still was time to act. You say you love your children above all else, and yet you are stealing their future in front of their very eyes.

Until you start focusing on what needs to be done rather than what is politically possible, there is no hope. We can't solve a crisis without treating it as a crisis. We need to keep the fossil fuels in the ground, and we need to focus on equity. And if solutions within the system are so impossible to find, maybe we should change the system itself. We have not come here to beg world leaders to care. You have ignored us in the past and you will ignore us again. We have run out of excuses and we are running out of time. We have come here to let you know that change is coming, whether you like it or not. The real power belongs to the people. Thank you.

—Dimitrios Roussopoulos, with Nathan McDonnell. Reviewed by Steve Lee, Dionysos Sephalophor, Bruce Wilson.

PREFACE

This book was originally published by Black Rose Books in 1993. Since then, the environmental crisis has become far more severe so that apocalyptic headlines are now a normal part of daily life. The seriousness of climate change, the most popularised of the environmental death knells, has become almost cliché and its manifestation multiplied into the previously unheard of phenomena of disaster, pestilence, famine and war.

The primordial permafrost is melting for the first time in millennia and islands are disappearing into the Pacific; heat waves kill thousands in South Asia and storms unleash ferocious violence in tropical areas; while summer bushfires are striking with heightened fury, the northern hemisphere witnesses either extreme or uncommonly mild winters; parasitical insects are invading new territories while indigenous peoples of the far corners of the Earth are forced to migrate to greener pastures.

Centre stage in the industrial causes of climate change is the extractivist mania for the fossilised remnants of primeval life; buried beneath the Earth, it is mined to fuel our economy and to service our attachment to plastics. In the same way as an addict goes to desperate measures, so this industry is resorting to increasingly dramatic terrains: war-torn Middle-Eastern deserts, the deep seas, the Albertan tar sands, shale gas trapped in fissures of rock and even the melting Arctic; the result is a web of pipelines, infernal landscapes, fracking-induced earthquakes, fierce civil wars and blackened tides.

Though less obvious than petroleum and mining industries, agriculture—and especially animal agriculture—also has an enormous ecological impact. The middle class fetish for a meat and dairy heavy diet is wiping away forests for animal farms; the feeding of the cattle, pigs and sheep requires an enormous quantity of crop and water resources while their excrements and flatulence are poisoning lands, rivers, sea and sky. Similarly, while oceans are being emptied of fish, chickens are condemned to horrific lives in cages. Our fruit and vegetables are being genetically manufactured in disturbing laboratories and are subjected to a salvo of new herbicides, pesticides and insecticides, while at the same time monocultures are wiping away the diversity of agriculture.

This ecological crisis is often manifested in dramatic events. The fallout from the explosion at the Fukushima nuclear reactor has meant not only the growth of mutant daisies near the site but the travelling of radioactive water across the Pacific Ocean, possibly explaining the scores of sea lions dying off the west coast of the USA. In the wake of the 2010 Gulf of Mexico oil spill, once green archipelagos that housed vibrant bird colonies are now poisoned skeletons, mangroveless black wastelands eroding and even disappearing under rising tides.

Clearly, the moment is grave; these are uncertain and alarming times. As the fact of the environmental crisis has come clearer into focus, there have been increasing attempts to throw together a response, among them new political parties, "corporate social responsibility," single-issue environmental organs of various stripes, green consumerism and the emergence of 'green capitalism'. Yet such attempts remain as a kind of politically unfocused groping that has, despite small victories, so far overwhelmingly failed to stem the crisis. Moreover, as predicted in the 1993 edition of this book, the state management of the environment, along with the rigamarole of intergovernmental institutions and agreements, has been pathetically insufficient.

There is, thus, now more than ever before, a need for clarity and coherence in understanding the nature of the crisis, its deeper roots in an economic system of greed and competition, and its intimate connection to the plethora of other crises of society. Likewise, what is necessary is an imagination of possibilities, a real of the extraordinary power for change when ordinary people in their neighbourhoods and cities organise together to fight the dominance of a violent and unjust system, and to envision a democratic and ecological society. Such a vision is certainly informed and nourished by the present success of many communities and their innovative projects; they are signs of a new world. The objective before us, as articulated in the tradition of social ecology, is the deepest possible transformation of the system and social relations, a fundamental decentralisation of political, economic, cultural and social power.

We have to face the raw brutality of capitalism, whether it is named neo-liberalism, corporate capitalism, state capitalism, state socialism, industrial capitalism, finance capitalism, or market capitalism—these are all different faces of the same system which, along with the repressive power of the state, has to be replaced root and branch. The environmental crisis is rooted in the nature of our society, in capitalism and the state. Having stated this, we also have to take into account that, historically, the social and ecological crisis preceded modern capitalism; thus, beyond even capitalism as an economic system, domination, hierarchy and exploitation *as such* must be erased. Fundamental change of this kind requires grassroots movements that are locally based in neighbourhoods and cities yet converge and coordinate confederally at a global level. Such struggles, multi-issued as they should be, must transcend narrow identity politics and the fragmentation of social movements and society generally, building community in a profound and creative way. These are the elements of what is meant by radical social change—root and branch.

This book has been brought back into print to answer a need for direction and coherence, for a program of political ecology that can confront and radically transform the ecological crisis as well as the concomitant economic, social, political and spiritual crises. Given the evolving times and changing questions, the book has been substantially renovated and even bears a more radical and urgent tone.

Section One has been preserved for its useful history of the State's attempt to manage the environment crisis. The same goes for Section Two, which gives a panorama of different responses to the ecological catastrophe. A note has been inserted at the beginning of these two chapters to remind the reader that these chapters were written in 1993 and have been preserved as such.

Section Three has undergone significant change. First, it has lost its analysis of the history of the Green Party in France. Second, the discussion of social ecology, centering on the exceptionally innovative and pioneering thinker Murray Bookchin, has been greatly expanded; the original treatment of the philosophy of social ecology has been supplemented with a scathing critique of mainstream environmentalism, exemplified by the NGOs, and its failure to question the capitalist system. This revised edition continues with an explanation of social ecology's praxis as libertarian municipalism and communalism (or what Öcalan terms 'democratic confederalism') in order to create an alternative society to replace capitalism; in such a project, emphasis is made on the place of radical community in forming democratic neighbourhoods and cities.

The completely new Sections Four and Five then follow. Section Four is concerned most of all with crystallising social ecology into a concrete road map. This begins with an outline of the city as central to the global economic system, its crisis and thus its alternatives. Two striking examples of successes inspired by social ecology are presented, the first in the Montreal downtown neighbourhood of Milton-Parc and the second in Rojava, the Kurdish majority area of war-torn Syria.

This Section concludes with a brief discussion of the Right to the City movement.

Section Five opens with a portrait of these extreme times, cataloguing the grave reports and incidents emerging solely in the first half of 2015, the year when this book was first being revised. This follows with a strong critique of, and a rousing challenge to the environmentalists and the Left in general, a call to arms that, alone, is pregnant with stimulating thought. In addition to the epilogue to the 1993 edition, a new epilogue has been added in light of the Eurozone's dramatic bullying and financial colonialism of Syriza-ruled Greece, a demonstration of the power of the system that an ecological movement must confront and transform.

Finally, a post-script has been added to debrief the COP21 climate change conference in Paris in December 2015, which this author participated in. Both analytical and anecdotal, this chapter ranges from the diplomat-infested negotiating rooms to the social movements on the streets.

July 2016
Nathan McDonnell
Dimitri Roussopoulos

SECTION ONE

The State Management of the Environment

It is by now commonly acknowledged that we are in the midst of an increasingly acute ecological crisis. We are in fact jeopardising the very survival of the human species, as well as other life forms on our planet. It remains an open question as to how we are to how we are to understand this crisis and embark on an effective course for change before it is too late.

Human misuse of the environment is not a new phenomenon. As many as 4,200 years ago, for example, Sumerian cities were deserted by their populations because the irrigated soil which produced the world's first agricultural surpluses became saline, waterlogged and eventually desertified by climate change. Plato is recorded complaining of the deforestation of the hills of Attica as a result of trees being cut for fuel and because of soil erosion due to overgrazing. There were warnings about crop failure and soil erosion as a result of animal husbandry practices as far back as first century Rome. Shipbuilding by Byzantines, Venetians and Genoans cut away large tracks of coastal forest around the Mediterranean. Coal-burning caused so much air pollution in the 1660s that London commentators complained bitterly. There was speculation about acid rain in the 1600s, which was scientifically confirmed by the 1850s. The current population debate dates back to work done by Sir William Petty in the mid 1660s, to be picked up again by Thomas Malthus some one hundred and fifty years later.

It was only with the capitalist industrial revolution, however, that the endemic ravage of nature began, and with it a measure of public concern. The theory that industrialism is unsustainable because of its excessive strains on the natural environment was put forward over a century ago, in the works of the geographer and anarchist philosopher Peter Kropotkin.[1] And in the nineteenth century, too, wilderness protectionists and conservationists began speaking out in several countries. As the natural sciences revealed more of the workings of nature and of the deleterious effects of the relentless subjugation of the natural world, alarm grew on the part of a small, informed public. This interplay of accumulating scientific knowledge and informed opinion developed steadily until after the Second World War, when awareness of environmental problems began to extend to the broader public. By the 1960s, the environment became the focal point of a social movement.

The first comprehensive air pollution law in the world was passed in Britain in 1863. The law also brought into being the first pollution control agency. More than one hundred years later, only 12 such agencies had been created. Today such agencies exist in the vast majority of nation-states. In 1886, the first international environmental agreement was signed; in 1993, there were over 250 agreements, most of them concluded since the 1960s. Since the 1972 United Nations conference on the environment in Stockholm, almost all important international bodies, from the Organisation for Economic Cooperation and Development to the World Bank, have adopted environmental protection programs. In the two decades following the Stockholm conference, some 10,000 new environmental groups have come into being adding to some 15,000 that had been formed prior to the conference.

Before the Second World War

Environmental awareness grew gradually among wider segments of the public as scientific evidence accumulated and the immediate effects of pollution, the loss of woodlands, and other forms of environmental degradation became clearly visible.

As we have noted, insight into how nature functions and into the relationships between all life forms goes back centuries. Just before he set sail for the Americas in 1799, the naturalist Alexander von Humboldt wrote that he sought "to discover the interaction between the forces of nature and the influence that environmental geography has on plant and animal life." But the nineteenth century was a turning point in the development of environmental awareness. In 1823, Jacques

Arago observed with alarm the destruction of giant trees in the Pacific which had taken hundreds of years to grow; while in 1832, George Catlin, a lawyer and painter of aboriginal people in North America, expressed great concern at the decline of the buffalo, which were vital to the survival of these people, and demanded a government policy to establish national parks. In 1859, Isidore Geoffroy-Saint-Hilaire, a professor at the Museum of Natural History and at the Faculty of Science in Paris, defined a new discipline devoted to: "the study of the relationship of organised beings in the family and society, and in their wholeness (aggregate) and community." He called this discipline 'ethology'.[2] In the same year, the German biologist Ernest Haeckel used the term 'ecology' to describe "the science of the relationships between organisms and the environment in the largest sense, taking all conditions into consideration." Again during the same year, Charles Darwin in England raised questions about the relationship between animals and plants, illustrating the problem with his renowned example of the drone bee and the clover patch.

A decade later, Ernest Haeckel gave a lecture in Jena, Germany, refining his first definition of ecology to encompass "the economy of nature" and "the research of all the relations between animals and their environment, inorganic and organic, which implies both amicable and hostile relations with animals and planets with which these are in direct or indirect contact."[3] In 1864, George Perkins Marsh published *Man and Nature or Physical Geography as modified by Human Action*, a pioneering study of the Mediterranean basin that included prescient observations of environmental deterioration. In 1877, the geographer and anarchist teacher Elisée Reclus warned of the degradation of the environment by human beings in his celebrated *Nouvelle géographie universelle*. In 1855, Wladimir de Schoenefeld, a founding member and Secretary General of the Société Botanique de France, wrote eloquently in the Fontainebleau Forest about the despoliation of the environment and its effect on many species.

The Origins of Environmentalism

The term 'environmentalism' is used in this text to refer to an approach that, like acute care medicine, deals with crises only as they arise and not with the underlying or systemic causes; in this sense, it is reactive rather than preventive. It also tends to assume that the best we on this planet can do is to survive, ignoring the potential for a creative and fruitful symbiosis between human beings and nature in a new kind of society. Within the environmentalist current are the preservationists, who essentially want to protect things as they are, a view that ignores the importance of dynamic balance or homeostasis.

A part of this current grew into conservationism, which promotes the carefully planned use of natural resources—both biotic and abiotic—and elements of our historical heritage in order to ensure that no unnecessary harm is done to them. It seeks to ensure the continued survival of particular resources such as areas of land or species of wildlife. These elements contribute a subtle conservatism to environmentalism: it is concerned with the environmental crisis but not with a systemic transformation of the social and economic structures that produce this crisis. Thus, it tends to be biased toward the concerns of the elite, proposing reforms that will make life more pleasant for the already privileged, but neglecting the problem of social and economic inequality.

The development of the discipline of natural history brought to light our civilisation's exploitation of nature. Among one segment of society there arose a growing concern for the protection of wildlife, followed by demands for the preservation of sectors of rural areas in order to offset increasing urbanisation. In Britain, the growth of botany, zoology, and natural history generally, from the sixteenth century forward, created the foundations of environmentalism in that country. The work of people like Gilbert White, Thomas Bewick, Carl von Linné, John Ray, Charles Darwin, and Alfred Russel Wallace all contributed, along with the poetry of William Wordsworth, to an environmental awakening.

In Victorian times, the study of natural history was thought to bring one closer to God, as well as providing the tools to conquer nature with science and technology. Progress meant mastery over nature. The work of Darwin, however, offered support for the view that natural evolution placed human beings and other species in the same sphere, and that this kinship enjoined humans to protect the environment from abuse.

By the 1880s, there were hundreds of natural history associations in England with thousands of members. At about the same time in France, the French Association for the Protection of Nature (SNPN) and the French Federation of Associations for the Protection of Nature (FFSPN) were founded.

The same morality infused in the anti-slavery movement also influenced British environmentalism. The year 1824

The State Management of the Environment

witnessed the establishment of the Society for the Prevention of Cruelty to Animals. The British Parliament passed laws to protect sea birds (1869), wild birds (1872), and wild fowl (1876). On the continent, a convention took place in Berlin in 1885 on fishing salmon in the Rhineland and an international convention was held in Paris in 1895 with the goal of establishing protection for birds. Opposition to the killing of birds for the plumage used in fashionable clothing and hats was led by women in the mid 1880s and their protest led to the founding of a variety of organisations in Britain and the colonies. The feather boycott resulted in the passage of legislation against trade with India in such wildlife and ultimately in the banning of such exports from India by the colonial government.

In 1893, the National Trust was established to acquire country land to protect Britain's cultural and natural heritage from the spread of industrial towns. Capitalism was having a devastating impact on urban social conditions and many critics including Charles Dickens and Friedrich Engels were depicting its negative effects on human health, on moral and social values, and on the physical environment. The protection of certain urban commons and rural areas was intended to make such space available for public use, as well as to preserve plants and animals.

The science of forestry was most advanced in Germany at this time and it played an important role in the growth of conservationism worldwide. British colonialism in India was bent on the profitable exploitation of India's forests to enhance state revenues. As early as 1847, the British brought in German foresters to pursue this objective. But in Australia, also a British colony, no such scientific management was engaged and clear cutting was imposed in the most rapacious manner. During the 1660s in Africa—and especially in southern Africa—European colonialism resulted in the reckless clearance of forests, the rapacious killing of animals for skins and other treasures (for example, hippopotamuses for their teeth, rhinoceroses for their horns, elephants for their ivory and ostriches for their feathers). By the nineteenth century, certain protective measures were enshrined in law, with limited effect. In the early 1870s, 2,500 elephants were hunted down, yielding 50 tons of ivory, and in the single year of 1876 some 900 were killed. Some game reserves were established, like the Kruger National Park, but the effect was marginal. During the same period, soil erosion, drought and associated problems were observed. However, the warnings that were issued were generally ignored unless profits were in peril.

In the USA by the 1700s roughly 200,000 hectares of woods were cleared for farming in New England.[4] Sixty percent of the forests of Massachusetts was cleared by 1880. In the pattern of settlement of the country was reflected the instrumental attitude toward nature that is so characteristic not only of capitalism but of the Judeo-Christian heritage, codified as humanity's God-given 'dominion' over nature.

The alarm was sounded by numerous scientists, from J.J. Audubon to John Muir, and by philosophers such as Ralph Waldo Emerson and Henry David Thoreau. But it was the publication in 1864 of George Perkins Marsh's book *Man and Nature* that precipitated the establishment of a national forestry commission. At the same time, the US Congress set aside certain areas for recreational enjoyment as part of its land management plan; for example, Yosemite Valley and the Mariposa Grove were conditionally given to the State of California.

A decade later in 1872, 800,000 hectares were set aside to create the Yellowstone National Park, the world's first such preserve. In 1879 the Royal National Park was established in Australia, in 1885 the Banff National Park in Canada, and in 1894 the Tongariro National Park in New Zealand. The motives for these laudable measures were mixed, ranging from national prestige, to wilderness preservation, to creating areas for public recreation.

By the 1900s a controversy had arisen in the United States between the preservationists influenced by British protectionism and the conservationists influenced by German forestry. The former wanted wilderness areas to be set aside for recreational and educational purposes only, while the latter wished to exploit nature rationally—read profitably. The protagonists in this debate were John Muir, the naturalist who founded the Sierra Club in 1892 (and who was something of a religious zealot in his literal worship of nature), and Gifford Pinchot, a wealthy student of German forestry who favored the planned commercial exploitation of woodlands. The conflict was confined to a narrow circle of professionals and self-appointed guardians of the public good, which often were conflated with their own particular interests.

A number of state management measures were introduced in the United States under the Republican presidency of Theodore Roosevelt. In 1907 the Inland Waterways Commission was established at the prompting of Pinchot who recognised the importance of hydroelectric power, water transportation, and flood and erosion control. The same year saw the creation of the National Conservation Commission headed by Pinchot. It was short-lived because of Congressional fear of growing presidential powers, prompting Congress to block his legislative agenda. Under Roosevelt, however, Pinchot was able in 1909 to organise the first North American Conservation Congress, which he chaired and which drew together delegates from Canada, Newfoundland, Mexico and the USA. This congress concluded that it was essential to approach conservation from a transnational perspective. Another effort to organise a meeting of countries extending beyond North America was shelved by President Taft whose more conservative Republican administration did not manifest the same interest in environmentalism as that of Roosevelt's.

The United States was not the only nation in which efforts were made to promote conservation. Conservationists elsewhere also sought to establish certain rules. In 1900 a conference for the protection of African mammals was held in London; in 1902 a convention on the protection of birds took place in Paris. But these gatherings expressed concern with protection primarily in the aim of serving human interests. The narrow anthropocentric character of the protectionist approach was reflected in the first international agreement to protect animals, which was signed in Vienna in 1868 and limited to the protection of those animals useful to agriculture and forestry. By 1902 this agreement had been signed by twelve European countries.

Furthermore, it was hunters and naturalists who sponsored the establishment in 1903 of the Society for the Preservation of

The State Management of the Environment

the Wild Fauna of the Empire, dedicated to the protection of animal life in the British colonies (the first such international organisation). For one of the most interesting examples of the conflict between the aims of wildlife preservation and those of the protection of animals central to human use, we must look to the period following the First World War. Almost half a million wild animals were killed in Southern Rhodesia alone in the post-war period because colonial authorities wanted to protect domestic stocks from disease as part of an anti-tsetse fly campaign.

Prior to the presidency of Franklin D. Roosevelt, conservationism had become associated with the capitalist interests around the Republican Party. But the Democratic Party in government was more sincerely committed to environmental protection. Using the power of the State to bring about economic recovery during the Great Depression, it created the Tennessee Valley Authority and the Civilian Conservation Corps, deploying the unemployed in flood control, forestry and soil erosion prevention efforts. Preservationism underwent a renewal under the Democratic administration. In 1934 almost seven million people visited national parks; four years later these parks attracted 17 million visitors. The federal State sought to create greater public access to the parks, which granted temporary psychological relief to the people of the overpopulated eastern states. Wilderness enthusiasts, however, objected to having more roads being built into the parks.

It was also during the Franklin D. Roosevelt years that the most massive environmental disaster to date occurred in the USA. Hundreds of dust storms ripped across the Great Plains, some blocking all sunlight and leaving six metre high drifts, driving dust from Texas to North Dakota. These storms were the result of over half a century of agriculture which ploughed long straight furrows and relied on a single crop, giving rise to the deterioration of sod—an important buffer to wind and drought—and leaving fields bare of vegetation. Some 1.3 million square kilometers of topsoil had been eroded and the country was forced to import wheat. In its 1936 report, the Great Plains Committee concluded that the single-minded pursuit of profits, unregulated competition, and the notion that nature could be completely subjugated to human will, would lead to a serious environmental disequilibrium.[5]

In Europe around the same time, the establishment of national nature organisations in France and Belgium in 1925-1926 and the creation of the Netherlands Committee for International Nature Protection revived calls for the establishment of a large inter-state body to address environmental concerns. By 1934, *l'Office international pour la protection de la nature* was established, but the initiative was derailed by the advent of the Second World War.

During the war years, some international consultation took place with the aim of planning for the conservation of natural resources and the re-establishment of a transnational organisation. The American conservationists stepped up their pressure, so that by 1944 there was recognition on the part of state agencies and the political parties that conservation would have to be an essential part of the new post-war world order. However, conflicting agendas impeded these efforts. For example, the basic aim of the Anglo-American Petroleum agreement was the development of world petroleum resources, whereas the new UN Economic and Social Council (ECOSOC) wanted energy conservation to be a key to postwar economic planning. The US State Department and the individuals around the Anglo-American petroleum deal pursued an essentially self-serving agenda, while the scientific circles around the United Nations were attempting to reflect broader interests.

After the United Nations

In spite of numerous setbacks and ideologically charged conflicts, the post-war period saw some real victories for the conservation movement. By 1946, the Americans were urging ECOSOC to convene a scientific conference in the United States to "consider the conservation and effective utilisation of natural resources." And in 1949, the United Nations Scientific Conference on the Conservation and Utilization of Resources (UNSCCUR) was held.

The Food and Agricultural Organization (FAO) of the UN was founded in Québec in 1945. It focused on the development and exploitation of natural resources with a view to solving nutrition problems by improving the production and distribution of food. FAO's earliest efforts reflected the limits of a conservationist perspective insofar as they were driven as much by the goal of controlling and managing world agricultural production as by broader humanitarian aims.

In the background loomed the politics of hunger, population and land. The Great Depression had given a renewed lease on life to the dire prognostications of Malthus. In the immediate post war period, books like *The World's Hunger* by Frank Pearson and

Floyd Harper, *Our Plundered Planet* by Fairfield Osborn, and *Road to Survival* by William Voght were published, meditating on the implications of unchecked population growth in conditions of limited resources; they wondered how the Earth could possibly meet the needs of a growing population. Voght, an avowed neo-Malthusian, became a bestseller. He insisted that the United States was self-indulgent, over-populated, wasteful and doomed. His warnings were soon eclipsed as the US economy burst into a boom of material production and consumption. However, Voght's assertion that the country was running low on resources did eventually lead to the founding in 1952 of Resources for the Future, an organisation heavily influenced by trade and business organisations that had their own particular angle on conservation.

International Efforts to Protect Nature

The Europeans, especially the Swiss, Belgians and Dutch, worried that the newly founded UN was disproportionately influenced by Anglo-American interests. A tug of war ensued over how to manage the environment, a struggle that lasted several decades. Europe was driven above all by a desire to progress through its postwar economic reconstruction and re-assert itself in the world economy.

From the International Office for the Protection of Nature (IOPN), to the founding in 1946 of the United National Educational, Scientific and Cultural Organization (UNESCO), the international politics of environmentalism was marked by struggles over what kind of growth to encourage and over whose interests growth would favor. There were some generational conflicts as well, with the older European school tending toward a preservationist approach, while many new American scholars favored more environmental research. There was also considerable vying for position, with various organisations each seeking to establish itself as the dominant environmental protection agency.

Among UNESCO's mandates was the promotion of international exchanges of scientific research. Interestingly, in 1947 UNESCO's Department of Natural Science began to research and circulate scientific data on the Amazon forest. At its general conference that same year, it took a small step forward when it expounded the idea that nature could not be divorced from culture and that the preservation of rare and interesting plants and animals was a vital part of scientific endeavor.

Also in 1947 IOPN facilitated the establishment of a Provisional International Union for the Protection of Nature (IUPN). Formally founded a year later, the IUPN sought to encourage cooperation in public education, regional planning, scientific research, preservation of wildlife and its habitats through the creation of protected areas, and scientific research bringing together governments, and concerned national and international organisations. Its constitution reveals an overlap between preservation and conservation perspectives. It was the dominant assumption of the organisation that nature existed to serve human ambitions and that conservation was meant to assist in the fulfillment of this goal.

Conservation efforts necessitated the gathering and compilation of the most complete information about the state of the environment on an ongoing basis. And it was to this end that the United Nations Scientific Conference on the Conservation and Utilization of Resources (UNSCCUR) was held in the USA in 1949. Jointly organised by UN agencies such as the World Health Organization (WHO), the Food and Agricultural Organization (FAO) and the International Labor Organization (ILO), the conference brought together a total of 500 delegates from some 49 countries (excluding the Soviet Union). Marked by an atmosphere of optimism about the unlimited power of science to discover and create new resources, the main purpose of this gathering was to take stock of and exchange information about natural resources. Every imaginable question was dealt with: fuels and energy, water, minerals, forests, interdependence of resources, food, and all applied technologies. Engaging in what they deemed politically neutral scientific discussions, participants at the conference assiduously avoided overtly political issues, although in the tense climate of the Cold War there were obvious questions that might have been raised about the potential and actual political benefits of the scientific research being conducted. But, in fact, most states did not regard this kind of conference as politically valuable; it was only when many governments began to develop environmental protection programs that such conferences took on greater political significance as with the Biosphere Conference in 1968 and the Stockholm Conference in 1972.

By the mid 50s scientists had come to dominate the IUPN. Dedicating itself, unlike UNESCO, primarily to the protection of nature, it changed its name in 1956, largely due to American pressure, to the International Union for Conservation of Nature and Natural Resources (IUCN), although the name change did nothing to alter the organisation's preservationist bias. In 1960 a twin body to IUCN was founded called the World Wildlife Fund (WWF), which was devoted to raising large sums of money for projects designed to protect wilderness and wildlife. A disproportionate amount of the money raised by this organisation was spent in North America and Europe; the other three continents received 15 per cent of the funds. Eventually, under criticism by donors for its Eurocentric approach, the IUCN began to sponsor projects to preserve areas of wild nature in Asia.

The colonial states of the northern hemisphere also retained an interest in the African environment in the post-colonial period. Indeed, conservationists were eager to encourage the new African states to conserve natural vegetation, soil, water, and natural resources. For instance, when the Third International Conference for the Protection of the Fauna and Flora of Africa took place, in Bukavu, (in the Belgian Congo) in 1953, the IUCN initiated the African Special Project and a series of studies and conferences were organised. The new national governments were told that they had to plan for the rational exploitation of nature, and that such planning would be conducive to international aid. Furthermore, the IUCN provided specialists to advise interested African states and drafted the agreement adopted in 1967 by the Organisation of African Unity (OAU) as the African Convention for Conservation of Nature and Natural Resources, which came into effect in 1969.

From the post-war period to the 1960s, then, conservation was clearly the reigning ideology of environmentalists and was given expression in a multiplicity of programs and projects.

The Road to Stockholm and Rio

By the late 1960s environmentalism had gained a good deal of momentum. Not only had the warnings of various writers had a decisive public impact, but accumulated scientific research and a series of environmental disasters pointed to a problem of increasingly alarming proportions.

In 1962, under the pen name Lewis Herber, Murray Bookchin published *Our Synthetic Environment*, a comprehensive examination of the deleterious environmental effects of industrial development and technology, from air pollution to contaminated milk and the misuse of chemical pesticides. Six months later Rachel Carson published *The Silent Spring*—a simpler text by contrast, focusing on the single issue of pesticides, and especially DDT. Although there had been forecasts of the potentially dangerous environmental impact of these products as far back as 1945, they did not gain the same wide public attention as Carson's message. *Silent Spring* was serialised in the New Yorker magazine and became a bestseller, selling over half a million copies in its cloth-bound edition alone. By 1963, it was published in 15 languages. It also became the target of criticism in official political and corporate circles, as both state authorities and industry feared the public outcry the book aroused. But Carson's was only the first of a series of works on environmental degradation to gain a wide public hearing. Her basic message was echoed in the United States by Paul Ehrlich, Barry Commoner, Lamont Cole, Eugene Odum, Kenneth Watt, and Garret Hardin. The cumulative effect of the work of these pioneers on public consciousness was palpable; on April 22nd 1970, the largest demonstration in history calling for the protection of the environment took place when roughly 300,000 Americans turned out to mark Earth Day.

In 1972, *The Limits to Growth* was published. This report had its roots in the 1940s and the seminal studies of Jay Forrester, an academic at the Massachusetts Institute of Technology. Forrester devised a forecasting methodology that had applications in the areas of digital computers, tactical military decision-making and information-feedback systems, as well as studies of the interacting forces of social systems. But the 1972 report was an initiative of the Club of Rome, an organisation of technocrats, scientists, economists, politicians and industrialists from 25 countries. A precursor to the Trilateral Commission,[6] its objective was to study the emerging global system in all its aspects—political, environmental, social, and economic. Forrester's work at MIT was used to develop the global modelling techniques employed in the writing of the report.

The Limits to Growth contributed to conservationism the idea that the environmental crisis is rooted in exponential economic growth. The report predicted that by the end of the century the cumulative effects of pollution, food shortages, and the exhaustion of natural resources would spell disaster. Among the remedies it proposed were a 40 per cent reduction in the birth rate, a 40 per cent reduction in industrial investment, a 20 per cent reduction in agricultural investment and a substantial transfer of wealth from the rich countries to poor ones.

The Limits to Growth had its parallel in Britain in *Blueprint for Survival*, which was also based on the premise that the combined effects of continuing population growth and the depletion of natural resources demanded changes in human practices. However, while *Limits to Growth* was oriented toward government measures, *Blueprint* underscored the need for a re-evaluation of received attitudes at the base of society.

By the late 1970s, some four million copies of *The Limits to Growth* had been sold in 30 languages. But the conclusions of the report did not go unchallenged. For instance, researchers at the Science Policy Research Unit of the University of Sussex in Britain issued a report that drew attention to the weaknesses of the MIT methodology and to the ideological values underpinning the analysis. The crucial problem, they concluded, was to assure more equal distribution of wealth and resources, but rather than simplistically calling for an end to growth, they placed emphasis on the quality of development. And their report underscored the importance of future technical progress, including the development of nuclear power, without cautioning against this environmentally harmful technology.

The Limits to Growth was one of several studies to have a bearing on the UN Conference on the Human Environment held in Stockholm in 1972. In preparation for that conference, a research group at MIT produced a Study of Critical Environmental Problems (SCEP), which discussed the effect on global climatic and terrestrial conditions of specific atmospheric, terrestrial, and marine pollutants and examined research and monitoring methods. This study declared that, "Currently, and in the foreseeable future, the advanced industrial societies will have to carry the load of remedial action against pollution." It went on to call for a more complete enquiry into marine oil pollution, atmospheric carbon dioxide build-up, and the negative effects of supersonic transportation.

The urgent tone of academic studies was both spurred and borne out by a series of environmental disasters occurring between 1966 and 1972. Environmental crises were not, of course, unprecedented: in 1948, twenty people died and some 40 per cent of the population of Donora, Pennsylvania, became ill with the effects of sulfurous fog; in 1952 a winter fog in London resulted in the immediate deaths of 445 people, while an additional 4,000 people died mostly from long-term circulatory or respiratory disorders. (It took another four years before the Clean Air Act was passed by the British House of Commons.) In 1955 a fire started and burned for 85 hours at the Windscale nuclear power plant in northern England due to overheating. But it was from the beginning of the 1960s that the combination of mass media coverage and growing environmental consciousness intensified public awareness and concern.

In 1966 a pit-heap collapsed in Aberfan, South Wales, leaving 144 dead (116 of them children) bearing witness to the hazards of abandoned land and pollution. In 1967, the tanker Torrey Canyon spilled an estimated 875,000 barrels of crude oil off the southwest coastal tip of England. (In 1950, there was one oil tanker larger than 50,000 dead weight tons; a decade later, there were over 600 tankers heavier than this.) The use of detergents to break down the oil caused further biological deterioration of the environment. The event shook public opinion to the extent that two years later a Royal Commission on Environmental Pollution was struck and two agreements were signed: the Convention Relating to Intervention on the High Seas in Cases of Oil Pollution Casualties and the Convention on Civil Liability for Oil Pollution Damage. In 1969 an oil blowout on a Union Oil Company platform off the coast of Santa Barbara, California caused great damage. It took two days to bring the blowout under initial control only to have it erupt again a few weeks later. The crisis lasted for weeks and months later beaches were still polluted. The US Secretary of the Interior ordered the immediate closing of all oil wells, but within 24 hours he allowed resumption of drilling and production.

In spite of laws and conventions, an estimated 10,000 annual spills of oil and other hazardous materials polluted the navigational waters of the United States alone during the late 1960s.[7] And by now all sorts of environmental catastrophes had begun to receive attention and come into public view: mercury pollution through chemical production in Minamata, Japan, leading to 857 deaths between 1953 and 1961; a gas explosion in Feyzin, France, in 1966 which left 45 dead; in 1976 in England at Windscale again 35 people died; in the same year in Seveso, Italy, 700 persons were evacuated due to dioxin poisoning; in 1978 in San Carlos, Spain, 200 people died due to an accident involving the transportation of gases; in 1979 200,000 people were evacuated at Three Mile Island in the USA as a result of nuclear reactor trouble; in the same year in Mississauga, Canada, a chlorine explosion after a train derailment required the evacuation of 220,000 people; in the same year, in Novosibirsk, USSR, emissions of chemicals left 300 dead; in 1979 an accident on an oil-drilling platform in the Gulf of Mexico caused oil spilling for nine months; in

1982, in Caracas, Venezuela, a petroleum explosion resulted in 101 deaths; in 1983, in Tacoa, an explosion of stored gas left 153 dead, and the casualty list continues…

Although there was no dearth of international meetings and conferences during this period, the Intergovernmental Conference of Experts on the Scientific Basis for Rational Use and Conservation of the Resources of the Biosphere held in 1968 under the sponsorship of UNESCO was of particular significance. Paving the way for Stockholm, more than a third of the recommendations of this conference called for more environmental research and education.

But the culminating point of the growing recognition of the importance of state management of the growing environmental crisis was the United Nations Conference on the Human Environment, held in Stockholm in 1972. This conference also revealed a perceived need to absorb or co-opt the energy of various lobbies demanding more environmental regulation before supporters of these campaigns became too political. As will be discussed later, the Stockholm conference led to the establishment of the United Nations Environmental Program (UNEP), which reflected the collective perspectives of the governments of the more powerful developed nations and sought to incorporate the less developed countries and their politicians and bureaucrats into global conservation plans.

Whereas the 1968 conference focused on the collection of scientific data documenting the environmental crisis, the 1972 Stockholm conference shifted the inter-state agenda to the related political, economic and social problems. The conceptual framework of the conference was laid out in a report entitled Only One Earth produced a year earlier by

Baroness Jackson of Lodsworth, the former assistant editor of The Economist, Barbara Ward, and an American biologist, Rene Dubos. This report was reviewed by 152 consultants from industry, science, and the academy. A rather dry and uninspired document, Only One Earth observed that pollution, the waste and misuse of land, the consumer society, urban sprawl, and the exhaustion of natural resources were "problems of high technology" of the developed countries, whereas the problems of population, industry and pollution, chemicalised agriculture and urban growth were issues facing the less developed countries. The report was actually published by the International Institute for Environmental Affairs (IIEA) established by the Aspen Institute of Humanistic Studies in Colorado and chaired by Robert O. Anderson, head of the Atlantic Richfield oil company. After Stockholm the IIEA moved to London where it was headed by Barbara Ward.

The Stockholm conference gathered together representatives of 1 nation-states, 19 intergovernmental agencies, and 400 other intergovernmental and non-governmental organisations. With the exception of Romania, the Soviet bloc was absent, supposedly because there was no agreement on the voting status of the German Democratic Republic. China, however, was present.

Political representatives from developing nations insisted that environmental protection must be balanced with economic development and growth. They looked askance at any measures that might impede the development of industrial capitalism and its attendant benefits at home. Both state environmental managers and the lobbyists from the NGOs had to agree that conservationism had to take an equitable form.

The US government, itself, played a perniciously obstructive role in the Stockholm conference. It sponsored a ten-year moratorium on commercial whaling, but opposed many positions advanced or supported by Third World delegations. The American delegation sought to weaken the proposed International Register of Potentially Toxic Chemicals, abstained from voting against nuclear weapons testing, and generally sought to dilute the substance of any UN environmental program. Outside the meeting rooms the US government was condemned for its war in Indochina and the human and environmental costs of that war.

The UN organisers sought to confine the environmentalist NGOs to an official Environmental Forum, designed, as many activists noted, to divert their attention away from the official proceedings and thus prevented certain NGOs from asking controversial questions. Anticipating such a manoeuvre, the Swedish-based Pow Wow group had, in advance, organised a Folkets Forum (People's Forum) in 1971 in parallel. It expressed concern at the apparent neglect by the official conference of such critical issues as chemical and biological weapons production and the ecocide resulting from the US war in Indochina.

The underlying assumption of the participants in the People's Forum was that the official conference was enmeshed in irreconcilable contradictions because state representatives were beholden to vested interests in industry and government who stood to suffer from any far-reaching measures to stem the environmental crisis.[8] Not surprisingly, the NGOs had a very limited influence on the Stockholm conference, and in subsequent years many of these organisations concentrated on the work of public education and consolidating and extending their respective bases of support. In 1974, only about 150 NGOs attended the meeting of the Governing Council of UNEP (Stockholm's follow-up structure) and by 1980 there were only 20 represented. By 1982 the UN Environmental Liaison Centre listed some 2,230 environmental NGOs in less developed countries, a 60 per cent increase since Stockholm, and some 13,000 in developed countries, a 30 per cent increase since that meeting. After 1972 there was greater contact among NGOs across the world and more concerted action, giving form to a new political internationalism. These bonds were strengthened with increasing evidence of the ineffectuality of governmental action despite the pious rhetoric of 1972.

As the ruling interests became aware of the costs of the far-reaching changes necessary to protect the environment they attempted to divert attention away from the environmental crisis by focusing attention on the 1973-1974 energy crisis, declining economic rates of growth, and the unstable international situation symbolised by the Cold War. But as concerned citizens sought a deeper understanding of the environmental crisis, they developed a more holistic approach to environmental problems. There was a growing awareness among citizens that environmental problems were related to specific forms of economic and social organisation, including the political structure of the state. The limited and limiting perspectives of preservationism and conservationism began to be transcended; the epoch of ecology was beginning;

and the environmentalists who were not careerists and opportunists were rapidly learning from each other and creating more organisational links and networks.

In sum, the Stockholm conference had produced little more than a Declaration, a list of Principles and an Action Plan that represented an initial accommodation between the interests of the developed and less developed nation-states. The Stockholm conference was to be followed by a conference on population in 1974, on desertification in 1977, and on new and renewable energy sources in 1981. But Stockholm however did result in one notable political achievement: the establishment of the United Nations Environment Program (UNEP) 1972-1982, located in Nairobi, Kenya.

This body was composed of an international council for environmental programs, a secretariat to promote coordination within the UN system, and an environmental fund to which nation-states would voluntarily contribute monies.

UNEP created Earthwatch with a mandate for environmental management: that is, comprehensive planning in support of nature protection to preserve biological diversity. UNEP also helped to negotiate international agreements, such as the Bonn Convention on migratory species, the Convention on International Trade in Endangered Species of Wild Fauna and Flora, the Convention for the Protection of the Mediterranean Sea against Pollution (1976), the moratorium on whaling, among others and so on. Further, it set up an early warning system for environmental hazards and a system for reporting on the status of certain natural resources. Thus a process of regular reporting on environmental research, monitoring and assessment was initiated. The UNEP mandate also included education, public information and the training of environmental managers.

UNEP initiated the Mediterranean Action Plan, adopted by 16 nations located around the sea, which was designed to manage problems of pollution and coastal degradation. Similar regional action plans included the Red Sea (1976), the Kuwait area (1978), the West and Central African coast (1981) and the South-western Pacific (1982).

UNEP failed in its campaign against desertification (the degradation of land through human misuse resulting in the loss of fertility). Desertification is in part the legacy of colonialism, which forced subject nations to increase exports to meet the needs of the metropolises more cheaply and to pay taxes, thus pushing peasants into cash crop farming. This pressure to export continued when the new nation-states became part of the international capitalist economy as debtors so that indigenous agricultural practices were further undermined, reducing soil fertility, increasing soil erosion and engendering mass human impoverishment. One-third of the Earth's land mass is semi-desert but still supports more than 600 million people; half of this land supporting 80 million people is thought by scientists to be in the process of complete desertification. Solutions to desertification were known in the 70s, but they represented a threat to various powerful interests and hence the economic and political obstacles were insurmountable for UNEP. Its projects failed with the result, for instance, that deforestation, overgrazing, and poorly designed and managed irrigation led to the drought in the Sahel 1968-1973 and later the Ethiopian famine of 1984-1986.

The State Management of the Environment

From the spring of 1984, when the media reports started appearing about Ethiopia, public fund-raising efforts began to multiply. By 1986 more than $100 million was raised by pop and rock musicians with the Band-Aid and Live-Aid concerts, and another $51 million by the USA for Africa. Meanwhile the 1984-1986 famine spread to 20 countries and an estimated one million people died, 10 million abandoned their homes and lands looking for water, food, and fertile land. The Western media, the main transmitter of information about the famine, hardly acknowledged that environmental degradation was the root cause of the crisis, much less that this resulted from ecologically unsound development plans largely imposed on the south by the ruling interests in the North. But even the extremely circumspect World Bank quietly admitted in 1984 that Africa's development policies had to change.

In October 1984, the UN initiated World Commission on Environment and Development held its inaugural meeting chaired by the social democratic prime minister of Norway, Gro Harlem Brundtland. In 1987, the commission published the report *Our Common Future*, which examined trends in, among other things, energy, food, industry, international economic relations and human settlements, and offered forecasts for the beginning of the new millennium.

The Brundtland report augured the era of sustainable development. There was little actually new in the concept of sustainable development; foresters in Germany and India in the previous century and Pinchot, among others, at the beginning of our own century, advocated the need to manage natural resources rationally. What the now trendy term 'sustainable development' implied was that many opinion-making environmentalists could now approve of economic growth on the condition that environmental considerations were integrated into economic development plans.

Again and again the report called for better management. It also gave added impetus to the charge long advanced by the peace movement that the ongoing international arms race was a wasteful drain on human, financial and material resources that could otherwise be devoted to development and environmental protection.

Predictably, the recommendations of the Brundtland report were largely ignored, as their implementation would conceivably imperil the international economic system of industrial capitalism and its concomitant political structures.[9]

Twenty years after Stockholm to the month, 178 nation-states and 117 heads of states—35,000 people in all, including 9,000 journalists—attended the United Nations Conference on Environment and Development, otherwise known as the Earth Summit, in Rio de Janeiro, Brazil. It is worth noting that this supposedly auspicious conference took place in the same city where, as Amnesty International reported, street children were being shot to death by vigilante groups—often composed of off-duty police officers—paid by local businessmen to clear the streets of 'nuisances.'

The Earth Summit unfolded in a carnival-like atmosphere, and many observers ultimately decried it as a non-event, a missed opportunity. Few were naive enough to have believed that the conference would accomplish anything of substance, even with respect to the minimal goal of managing the environmental crisis. And the skepticism has been given ample

The State Management of the Environment

justification in the year that has elapsed since the conference.

Once again parallel to the official summit—and of greater significance in the long run—were the meetings of thousands of environmentalists and ecologists from NGOs from around the world. Together they worked on a remarkable collection of alternative international treatises and established transnational networks for future work. This time the entire spectrum of this new social movement was present, from New Agers to representatives of the Green political parties.[10]

The Earth Summit gave rise, of course, to the adoption of "The Rio Declaration," which enshrined the objective of sustainable development. But its 27 principles, a kind of green human rights charter, are couched in vague terms and difficult to translate into action. They are so broad and abstract as to constitute little more than a pious wish.

Then the Convention on Biodiversity was adopted. It sought to protect endangered flora and fauna and declares that each nation-state will undertake its realisation. No timetable is indicated. The document accords the countries of the northern hemisphere a free hand in the biologically diverse regions of the southern hemisphere in exchange for royalties paid for all commercial exploitation and access to new biotechnologies and all products resulting from such research. The majority of countries signed this convention, the USA being a notable exception.

A convention on climate ought to have been given top priority. Before Rio, the European Community had proposed an 'ecotax' on energy and on CO_2 emissions as a step toward combating global warming. One of the preconditions was that the Americans and Japanese also accept this policy. The US refused, however, and hence the proposal was shelved. So the most ambitious plan for the Earth Summit dissolved into an unenforceable moral commitment to stabilise CO_2 emissions by the year 2000.

A proposed Convention on Forests was reduced to a mere declaration because, in the name of national sovereignty, several exporters of tropical wood (Brazil, India, Malaysia, and Indonesia) refused to be bound by it. Both producers and consumers are now simply requested to respect the heritage of the world's forests. As long as sustainable management is followed the logging of endangered species of trees can continue.

Agenda 21, a program of more than 800 pages, invited the rich countries to help the poor ones along the path of sustainable development. In order to allow for a series of priority actions (drinkable water, reforestation, reversing soil erosion, among others), the more developed countries were pushed to increase international development aid to 0.7% of their Gross National Product (GNP)—a step they had been promising to take since 1970. But only the Scandinavian countries, the Netherlands, Luxembourg, and the UK have, by 2017, accomplished this objective. Thus, the Rio Earth Summit also passed into history.

The first environmental agreements in history were a series of bilateral treaties for marine fisheries initiated in 1351 by England with Castile, Portugal, France and Burgundy. The first multilateral environmental treaty would come in 1857 regarding the navigation of Lake Constance, the first in a series of agreements regarding the Rhine River. The first

TABLE 1

International conventions, protocols, treaties and amendments relating to the environment: 1911–1983

Subject	Year signed							
	1911-20	21-30	31-40	41-50	51-60	61-70	71-80	81-83
Pollution, including marine	—	—	—	—	1	5	19	6
Marine/fisheries	—	—	—	3	8	4	10	5
Nature and resources	1	—	2	1	—	1	3	—
Toxic substances, including radiation	—	1	—	—	3	4	2	—
Animals	—	—	—	1	1	1	6	—
Regional development	—	—	—	—	1	2	4	—
Insects and pests	—	—	—	—	—	4	—	—
Plants	—	—	—	—	4	—	—	—
Ecosystems	—	—	—	—	—	—	2	—
Birds	—	—	—	—	1	1	—	—
Environments	—	—	—	—	—	—	1	—
Total	1	1	2	5	19	22	47	11

Source: United Nations Environment Program, *Register of International Treaties and Other Agreements in the Field of the Environment* (UNEP/GC/INFO/119 (Nairobi: UNEP, 1984).

state pollution agency was created some 150 years ago. In the 20 years preceding the 1987 publication of the Brundtland report, more than 130 nation-states established environmental agencies and more than 180 international agreements had been signed. (A 1984 UNEP register documents 108 international agreements (see Table 1) and a 1985 update lists 257 multilateral treaties.[11]) By 2017, there were 3390 international environmental agreements (classified as bilateral, multilateral or 'other') and an estimated ten million NGOs worldwide.[12]

How have all these efforts to promote the State management of the environment improved the ecological health of the Earth? The survey of the current state of the global environment in the following chapter would suggest that the impact of these initiatives has been far too limited.

At the Rio Summit, as the bureaucrats, politicians, and environmental managers were shaking hands good-bye, the departing ecologists at the alternative summit were reminding themselves of the ongoing tragedy in the Amazon, not far from Rio. We know how important tropical forests are to the Earth's ecology and that there is widespread public concern about these forests. Sixty per cent are found in sub-Saharan Africa and 33 per cent in Brazil. Recall who is behind Amazonian deforestation: twenty US multinational corporations, among them Union Carbide, Massey Ferguson, Chrysler, Ford and Bethel Steel; ten Japanese multinationals including Mitsubishi, Toshiba, Sony, Suzuki; six German multinationals, for example, Volkswagen and Bosch; five Italian multinationals, such as Ferrari, Fiat, Pirelli; three British multinationals; and the Swiss group Nestle. And the mineral riches from the largest iron ore mine in the world, the Grand Carajas project, have already been divided up, three hundred years in advance, between Japanese, West European, and US multinationals.

Yet these vulturous corporations were nowhere to be seen at the Earth Summit, even though they are the State's silent partners or, indeed, their shadowy puppeteers.

SECTION TWO

Citizens' Responses to the Plight of the Earth

The most dangerous threat to our global environment may not be the strategic threats themselves but rather our perception of them, for the most people do not yet accept the fact that this crisis is extremely grave.

US Vice-President Al Gore, 1992

By the end of the 1980s, few speeches made by the heads of state of the developed nations would fail to invoke the environmental crisis, and corporate executives began to declare themselves committed environmentalists. But it is one thing to establish international treatises, national laws, and environmental ministries and agencies;

it is quite another to effect the concrete changes in attitudes, practices and institutions necessary to resolve the ecological crisis. It is true that, to date, there have been environmental improvements, at least temporarily, in a few critical areas. But overall the scientific indicators paint a grim picture.

Despite the substantial growth of environmental awareness among people throughout the world, the health of the Earth continues to deteriorate at an unprecedented rate. Here we can only sketch the contours of the problem; more ample documentation is readily available in hundreds of reports and books published in many countries and in most languages.

From 1972, the year of the Stockholm conference, to 1993, deserts expanded by 120 million hectares, claiming more land than that under cultivation in Nigeria and China combined. This area is as large as the United States east of the Mississippi River. Thousands of plants and animal species have ceased to exist since 1972. Over 500 billion tons of topsoil was lost to the farmers of the planet, an area almost the size of the agricultural land of India and France combined. According to the National Coalition Against the Misuse of Pesticides, the USA is producing pesticides today at a rate thirteen thousand times faster than when *Silent Spring* was published.

By the end of the 1980s, the world's forests were reduced by an estimated 17 million hectares each year, up from 11 million hectares at the beginning of that decade. As the demand for lumber, paper, and firewood soared, and as the need for cropland increased, the pace of deforestation has been stepped up. Some countries, such as Ethiopia, Mauritania, Thailand and the Ivory Coast, have lost nearly all their woods.

Every year, some six million hectares of land are so

severely damaged that they are lost to production, becoming wasteland. Topsoil is lost to wind and water erosion, deforestation and over-grazing. Hundreds of cities are afflicted with persistent air pollution, and this problem is now affecting rural areas. Breathing air in some cities like Mumbai is equivalent to smoking 10 cigarettes a day, and in Mexico City it is considered life-threatening. Two million cars and the use of low-grade leaded gasoline in Bangkok have added 38 different chemicals to the city's air. In this same city in 1990, over 1 million people were treated for respiratory problems; lead poisoning has reached epidemic proportions among the city's children, while the incidence of lung cancer is three times higher in Bangkok than in the rest of Thailand.

In other parts of the planet, air pollution and acid rain damage crops and forests. Many European forests are already dead, others continue to deteriorate. In the northeastern part of North America, the sugar maple of Canada and the USA has been experiencing stunted growth for some years, and foresters have concluded that it is too late to reverse the process. As China now surpasses the USA as the world's leading coal burner, the damage to Chinese forests is massive. In his book *Earth in the Balance*, former US Vice-President Al Gore writes:

> Some of the successes in dealing with air quality have created new problems. For example, the use of tall smokestacks to reduce local air pollution has helped to worsen regional problems like acid rain. The higher the air pollution, the farther it travels from its source. Some of what used to be Pittsburgh's smoke is now

Labrador's acidic snow. Some of what Londoners used to curse as smog now burns the leaves of Scandinavian trees.

And while many of the measures that control local and regional air pollution also help reduce the global threat, many others actually increase that threat. For example, energy-consuming 'scrubbers' used to control acid precipitation, now cause the release of even more carbon dioxide (CO_2) into the atmosphere. A power plant fitted with scrubbers will produce approximately 6 percent more global air pollution in the form of CO_2 for each BTU of energy generated. Moreover, the sulphur emissions from coal plants partly offset, and temporarily conceal, the regional effects of the global warming these plants help to produce worldwide.[13]

The US Environmental Protection Agency (EPA) reported in 1988 that ground water in 39 states contained pesticides. In 1990, the agency reported some 100,000 violations of its water quality standards. The EPA now claims that almost half of all rivers, lakes and creeks are still damaged or threatened by water pollution. At least half the river water in Poland is too polluted for industrial use. South Korea's Naktong River has become a helpless victim of that country's massive industrialisation: in 1990 alone, some 343 factories illegally dumped toxic wastes into the waters. Thousands of people became violently ill in the city of Taegu when they consumed drinking water containing phenol, a chemical used in processing circuit boards for computers. The ocean explorer Jacques Cousteau claims that pollution in the oceans has now damaged the very thin membrane on the ocean's surface—

neuston—which helps capture and stabilise the food supply for the tiniest sea organisms, phytoplankton, thus beginning the food chain.

The effects of water pollution are the worst in the developing countries. More than 1.7 billion people do not have access to safe drinking water, causing death from cholera, typhoid, dysentery, and diarrhea from both viral and bacteriological sources. More than three billion people do not have proper sanitation systems and thus incur the risk of contaminated water. The huge Aral Sea basin in the former Soviet Union is virtually dead. The accumulation of agricultural pesticides in local water supplies causes birth defects, miscarriages, kidney damage, and cancer. The incidence of oesophageal cancer is seven times the national level. But this is only a fraction of the picture: a 1987 estimate calculated the Soviet Union's health costs at 190 billion rubles, or 11 per cent of the gross national product at that time.

In 1991, atmospheric measurements made by the US National Aeronautics and Space Administration indicated that the Earth's protective ozone layer is being depleted at twice the rate scientists had calculated, and by four to five per cent over the USA in a 13-year period. Research by scientists has recently concluded that 200,000 additional deaths from skin cancer could occur in the USA alone during the next 50 years. Al Gore writes:

> Of course, the history of climate change is also the history of human adaptation to climate change. During the subsistence crisis of 1816-1817, for example, the bureaucratic, administrative tendencies of the modern state were given

great impetus. In virtually every European country, central governments organised and distributed the scarce supplies of food and imported new stocks from Odessa, Constantinople, Alexandria, and America. For the first time, large-scale public work projects were organised chiefly to provide employment in the hope of staving off the popular disturbances and food riots that accompanied the subsistence crisis. In the 1930s, the Dust Bowl was among the many disruptive social and economic problems that led to an even more complex version of the administrative state, Franklin Roosevelt's New Deal.

All of these changes in climate patterns took place during temperature variations of only 1 to 2 degrees Centigrade. Yet today, at the close of the twentieth century, we are in the process of altering global temperatures by up to three to four times that amount and causing changes in climate patterns that are likely to have enormous impacts on global civilization. Among the most dramatic effects, if the historical record is any guide, will be massive migrations of people from areas where civilization is disrupted to other areas where they hope to find the means for survival and a better way of life—but with unpredictable consequences for those areas.[14]

The statistics that informed an international agreement to remove ozone-destroying chlorofluorcarbons (CFCs) by the year 2000 are now thought to be too conservative. It will still take decades for the upper atmosphere to recover. CFCs have been produced for fewer than 60 years and yet they have already had a dramatic effect on the atmosphere. What about the effect of mass production of the other 20,000 chemical compounds introduced every year? Few are extensively tested for environmental effects before being used, although, ironically, CFCs were.

During the 1980s, the amount of carbon pushed into the atmosphere from the burning of fossil fuels had reached six billion tons. The increasing concentration of this and other greenhouse gases, largely produced by industrial countries, is projected by scientists to rapidly increase global average temperature in coming decades.

At the local, regional and global levels the devastation of the biological diversity of the planet continues unabated. Biologists find it difficult to calculate accurately the number of plant and animal species that were lost during these last decades. The 2005 Millennium Ecosystem Assessment estimated that 10-30% of the mammal, bird and amphibian species are threatened with extinction; it has been predicted that one fifth of the species on Earth may disappear in the coming decades. What cannot be calculated at this time is how long such a rate of extinction can persist before ecosystems begin to collapse.

Since the Stockholm conference the world population has almost doubled: we were 3.8 billion people in 1973 and now, in 2015, we are 7.3 billion. During the same period the world economy has grown immensely, placing historically unparallelled demands on the Earth's limited resources.

The revolution in chemical production and use continues with awesome speed. In 1930, one million tons of chemicals were produced; in 1950, seven million tons; in 1970, 63 million tons; in 1990, 500 million tons. World production is doubling every seven to eight years. In the USA alone there are an estimated 650,000 commercial and industrial sources of hazardous waste. According to UNEP, more than seven million chemicals have now been discovered or created, and every year several thousand new ones are added. Of the 80,000 now in common use in large quantities, most produce chemical waste and most are hazardous. Many new chemical waste compounds are never tested for potential toxicity. The amount of this waste dumped into landfills, lakes, rivers, and oceans is staggering.

Industrial capitalism, in both its free-market and state capitalist guises, has created a civilisation of the mass production of garbage. In the USA alone, every person produced more than twice his or her weight in garbage every single day. The industrial countries are the greatest producers of garbage, but the mountains of garbage are also on the rise all over the world. Waste managers offer two basic solutions: landfills and incineration. Landfills are a limited option. Of the 20,000 US landfills in existence in the in 1979, more than 15,000 have since been closed, having been filled to permanent capacity. So waste managers are now busy promoting incineration. Again in the USA, almost always the trendsetter, municipal waste incinerated from 7 per cent in 1985 to over 15 per cent in 1989, and has continued to rise. Huge investments in new incinerators are underway, as companies producing nuclear reactors are switching products. According to US congressional investigators, the air pollution from incinerators typically includes dioxins, furans, and pollutants like arsenic, cadmium, chlorobenzenes, chlorophenols, chromium, cobalt, lead, mercury, PCBs, and sulfur dioxide. In a lengthy study about mercury emissions the US Clear Water Fund found that:

Municipal waste incinerators are now the most rapidly growing source of mercury emissions into the atmosphere. Mercury emissions from incinerators [have] surpassed the industrial sector as a major source of atmospheric mercury and are likely to double over the next five years. If the incinerators under construction and planning come online, with currently required control technology, mercury emissions from this source are likely to double. The growth will add millions of pounds of mercury to the ecosystem in the next few decades unless action is taken now.[15]

Toxic air pollution is only one part of the problem with garbage incineration. The new solid waste produced in the incineration process is in some ways an even more serious one. The some 10 per cent that remains as ash is highly toxic. Most municipalities do not treat this toxic ash as hazardous waste.

In 1992, the Royal Society of London and the US National Academy of Science for the first time issued a joint report that began by stating:

If current predictions of population growth prove accurate and patterns of human activity on the planet remain unchanged, science and technology may not be able to prevent either irreversible degradation of the environment or continued poverty for much of the world.[16]

Acknowledging that science and technology cannot ensure a better future unless population growth slows quickly and the world economy is restructured, this extraordinary statement had next to no impact on the proceedings at Rio although it was issued months before the Earth Summit. Technological optimism had underpinned the twentieth century's response to environmental problems. But now two of the world's important scientific organisations openly admit that we cannot rely on a 'techno-fix.' Clearly, the attempts at state management of the ecological crisis have yielded results that are questionable at best.

We must conclude that for a genuine reversal of global patterns to occur, more far-reaching political and economic changes in the dominant institutions of our society must be made. These fundamental changes must, moreover, be undertaken by our generation, as it may be too late for the next. It remains an open and urgent question whether this generation will indeed be willing and able to take the necessary action 'from below' that our ruling elites have demonstrated themselves reluctant to take. But especially in the last 30 years or so, many citizens of nations West, East, North and South have become acutely aware of the immediate and long-term consequences of environmental deterioration and have begun to organise in one fashion or another in response to the plight of the Earth. And it is precisely to the variety of forms of popular response to the environmental crisis that we may now turn our attention.

It was estimated that in 1983 the British environmental movement comprised some three million members (almost six per cent of the total population), making it the largest movement in that country's history.[17] Table 2 lists the mainstream environmental organisations in Britain and the USA. The table is, however, incomplete, failing to include thousands of national, regional and local organisations, some

TABLE 2

Membership of selected British and US environmental groups 1968–1984 (in thousands).

	1968	1972	1976	1980	1984
Britain					
Royal Society for the Protection of Birds	41	108	204	300	340
Ramblers Association	15	26	30	32	37
National Trust	170	346	548	1000	1460*
Council for the Protection of Rural England	16	25	28	29	30
Royal Society for Nature Conservation	35	75	109	140	180
Total	277	580	919	1501	2047
United States					
National Wildlife Federation	364	524	620	818	820
Sierra Club	68	136	165	182	348
Wilderness Society	39	67	91	50	65
National Audubon Society	66	164	269	400	450
Izaak Walton League	56	56	50	52	50
Total	593	947	1195	1502	1733

Source: This figure is based on information from Francis Sandbach, *Environment: Ideology and Policy* (Oxford: Basil Blackwell, 1980), 12; and *The Conservation Directory* (Washington DC: National Wildlife Federation, various years). *1982.

falling within the mainstream of the movement and others of a more radical character. Still, it provides some indication of the scope of the movement in the Anglo-American part of the world.

It is important to realise, moreover, that environmental activism is not a phenomenon exclusive to the advanced industrial nations. In 1983, Alan B. Durning estimated that there were 100,000 such organisations, with 100,000 million members in the developing nations alone. According to the same author,

> [In the Third World] people understand global degradation in its rawest forms. To them, creeping destruction of the ecosystem has meant lengthening workdays, failing livelihoods, and deteriorating health. And it has pushed them to act.[18]

The genesis of this new international social movement is of particular interest to those concerned and committed to its objectives. From about the mid-1960s into the 1970s a new generation of organisations emerged which created a tide that dragged along the older established organisations. The moralistic preservationists and the utilitarian conservationists now had to share the stage with the new activists who became skilled lobbyists and public opinion leaders. This new social movement was far from homogeneous, embodying a variety of ideological tendencies.

Like other social movements of the period, the new activism was a response to powerful historical forces developing before the 1960s. Substantial changes took place in industrial societies after the Second World War, which ushered in a period of intense economic growth resulting in more widespread material affluence and reinforcing a naive belief in perpetual and penalty-free economic expansion. A near pathological consumerism fed a reckless hedonism so that the United States, for instance, with six per cent of the world's population, was producing and consuming over one-third of the world's goods and services by 1979. And yet there was discontent, especially among youth. For in the midst of this affluence many ugly contradictions were apparent.

By the early 1960s three powerful movements had emerged. The American civil rights movement, the international nuclear disarmament movement, and the student and youth movement, or the New Left, which also cut across national boundaries. All of these movements influenced each other and helped to create other movements, filling out the agenda for social and political change. But the imminent danger of a Third World War, a nuclear war, was the single most galvanising force for millions of people. Beginning with mass protests against the testing of atomic bombs—from 1945 to 1962 a total of 423 explosions took place, with the United States leading in the number of tests—the movement expanded in scope, going on to oppose the arms race and later to organise against the war in Vietnam and the Soviet invasion of Czechoslovakia. Accompanying the fear of war, which was primary, was the growing fear of the health hazards and damage to the environment attendant upon military research testing and production.

The more radical New Left youth in turn began questioning and organising against a political and economic system that did not respond to demands for fundamental change. By the mid-1960s this movement was pounding on the doors of power in almost all industrial countries (such as the USA, Britain, Canada, France, Italy and Japan), central European countries (such as Czechoslovakia), Mexico and several Latin American countries. The politics of protest and radical organising were being learned everywhere and quickly. The clarion call was for "participatory democracy" from the campuses to society at large. The rise of student activism was accompanied by the development of a counter-culture including the back-to-the-land movement, which advocated a return to nature in protest against materialist consumerism. By questioning the dominant modes of existence, the counter-culture deeply affected attitudes among all strata of the industrial societies. This was also the period when more scientific information on environmental conditions began to be assembled and disseminated more widely and when environmental awareness was accelerated by a series of reported environmental disasters. By the end of the decade the movement against nuclear energy was rolling forward.

The motor force of the environment movement of the 1970s was the battle against the building of nuclear reactors in the United States, Canada, Britain, France, West Germany, among other countries. The ramifications of this burst of construction were obvious; people made the connections between nuclear energy production and the production of nuclear weapons, hazardous wastes, and the potential for accidents with devastating effects, especially on communities located in the vicinity of reactors.

Audiences of up to 10,000 would come out to hear speakers on various aspects of what was happening to nature. And on Earth Day in 1970, the largest demonstration in defense of the environment in history was held in the United States. By 1980, roughly seven percent of the American population, some 17 million people, were estimated to be involved in the movement, and an additional 55 per cent sympathetic to its aims.[19] Ruling elites did not remain blind to the growing public concern and soon enough environmental issues began to make their way into official political discourse. After the Conservative Party victory in Britain, the word 'environment' figured for the first time in the Queen's Speech in July 1970. President Richard Nixon's 1970 Address to Congress declared a new decade of environmental state policy. Thus a new mass movement had pushed its way onto the public scene, placing a new question at the top of the public agenda. And it had at its disposal a growing body of scientific evidence that could not be easily disputed.

In response to grass-roots pressure, the state moved into high gear. The Organisation for Economic Cooperation and Development in Europe reported that whereas from 1956 to 1960 only four environmental laws had been passed, there were 10 laws enacted between 1961 and 1965, 18 between 1966 and 1970, and as many as 31 from 1971 to 1975. Environmental programs and agencies were being created everywhere. The political aim underlying this spurt of official action was to calm the fears of the environmentalists and the concerned public and to confine the issue to manageable proportions. The established political parties expediently refurbished their programs and rhetoric hoping to capitalise on the popular energy.

The environmental movement was not, of course, all of a piece. One of the largest movements in human history, it took root in various countries and drew on diverse political traditions. It was bound therefore to comprise a variety of ideological tendencies. In the following pages we will look briefly at its major components in the North American context. As developments on this continent invariably have an influence on political life around the globe, the North American spectrum finds parallels elsewhere, especially in Europe.

Conservationism

Before and during the 1960s a number of organisations emerged such as The Nature Conservancy (affiliated to the International Union for the Conservation of Nature) and The Sierra Club, and other similar organisations that were largely composed of people who loved nature and wilderness, such as hunters and campers. They were concerned with preserving 'the great outdoors'. The advocacy of these organisations over the many years of their existence led to the establishment of various national parks as well as state/provincial parks in different parts of North America. These are being preserved by the state as part of a public policy of conserving our 'natural heritage'. Earlier we referred to this lobby as preservationists, but in North America they have become part of the conservationist movement. Conservationism has at least two wings. One holds a faith in the power of the market to solve problems; it believes that environmental problems can be assimilated to the larger problem of the 'correct' division of property in society and thus seeks to enlighten corporations. It is the contention of this school that if all the air, water, and land was privately owned, rights to pollute could then be sold at a market price, perfectly balancing industrial and environmental interests. It has been the policy of political conservationists like Reagan, Bush and Thatcher to sell rights to industry with the belief that market capitalism will regulate all. The other wing, which is represented in the USA, for instance, by the left-wing of the Democratic Party subscribes to the ideal of liberal democracy and advocates limited state regulation to deal with environmental problems. This branch of conservationism overlaps with the environmentalist current described below.

Environmentalism

The approach of environmentalism is to deal individually with one crisis after another. Environmentalists tend to concentrate on bringing about small but urgent changes to the present order of things. Taken alone, however, these intense but circumscribed efforts tend to draw attention away from the need for changes in society's basic institutions of power. The result is that the larger picture gets lost; the forest cannot be seen for the trees, as it were. The environmentalist school is informed by the tenets of current liberal philosophy, as exemplified by such organisations as the Natural Resources Defense Council, Greenpeace, Friends of the Earth, Pollution Probe, and The Sierra Club. Groups such as these believe in technical solutions to environmental problems and maintain that state policy must be changed to assure the passage of more protective legislation.

Although influenced by conservationism, environmentalists differ from the conservationists insofar as they are not opposed to and even encourage mass popular action as a means of bringing pressure to bear on the powers that be in support of their goals; they also espouse a wider range of environmental concerns.

Organised primarily at the national level, these groups tend to be highly professionalised, employing well-paid and trained staff, and hierarchical in structure; they rely on the organisational technique of mass mailings to thousands of people simultaneously; and they use refined legal and government/corporate lobbying techniques, instead of being grass-roots democratic membership organisations. They welcome financial contributions without paying too much regard to the source of donations. While most of their positions implicitly challenge the dominance of large corporations, they shy away from any overtly radical criticism of the political and economic system as such, partly in order not to alienate politicians and the corporate elites.

Environmental Populism

There are hundreds of thousands of self-avowed environmentalist groups across North America at the local level. These local groups have in turn exercised a significant influence on the voluntary sector, with the result that thousands of small local actions to improve the environment are taken by community organisations and other local associations ranging from the Boy Scouts to church groups. Local environmental groups usually focus their attention on specific environmental issues. Actions are organised against incineration or landfilling of municipal waste, the effects of acid rain, nuclear power plants, hydro-electric projects, the use of pesticides, and so on. Except for some trade unions which organise around occupational hazards at the workplace, these activists have few financial resources and they have few paid workers; they are usually community-based and may network with similar groups elsewhere.

While these groups have no defined ideology, they express anti-corporate sentiments, since they often confront profiteering by companies at the expenses of human health and needs. Their militancy is often undercut, however, by their own town's or city's dependence on jobs and taxes from the corporations they are fighting. These activist groups lack a global analysis of the ecology crisis and the need for a radical alternative to present state and corporate policies. They are often motivated by the NIMBY syndrome (not in my back yard). It is these activists who generally support alternative lifestyles from health food stores to 'green products,' and mobilise around annual Earth Day actions. They display all the right instincts, but rarely do they articulate a serious alternative politics.

Deep Ecology

Turning to the more radical popular responses to the environmental crisis, we find the deep ecologists. In spite of a large body of literature devoted to the theme of deep ecology, this current is difficult to define. It originates with the desire to go beyond conservationism and environmentalism but attempts to do so without articulating a new social and historical project. Often verging on anti-rationalism in its celebration of 'the Natural', it seeks to replace an anthropocentric ethics and politics with what is referred to as biocentrism. In this view, the Earth, personified as Gaia, is intrinsically valuable, that is, its value is not predicated upon its utility for human beings, and all life—animate or inanimate—is equal within nature. Deep ecologists hold that in order to reduce destructive human pressures upon the Earth, population growth must diminish. Some deep ecologists have argued that pre-industrial societies lived in harmony with nature and that it is European civilisation that has destroyed this relationship of equilibrium. As Michael Tobias has observed,

> Deep Ecology concerns those personal moods, values, aesthetic and philosophical convictions which serve no necessarily utilitarian, nor rational end. By definition their sole justification rests upon the goodness, balance, truth and beauty of the natural world, and of a human being's biological and psychological need to be fully integrated within it.[20]

There is some overlap between deep ecologists and New Age enthusiasts who are primarily concerned with changes in lifestyles, personal change, self-realisation and spirituality, rather than social and political change. There is also however the eco-guerilla version of deep ecology called Earth First! Activists in this organisation believe that most land in the United States should be returned to its pristine natural state, and consequently they have engaged in such acts as the sabotage of construction sites and equipment to stop lumber companies, as well as the spiking of trees with steel nails to stop trees from being cut, sometimes imperilling the lives of loggers. Some Earth First! activists have taken positions with racist implications, such as regarding famine as a 'natural' measure against overpopulation which should not be mitigated by human assistance.

Bioregionalism

According to the bioregionalists, the environment should be viewed as a collection of bioregions each possessing its own ecological integrity. All other political divisions such as national borders are considered arbitrary and artificial. In their view, society should be decentralised and all political and economic demarcations should correspond to bioregional boundaries.

Bioregionalism means living within the "limits and the gifts provided by a place, creating a way of life that can be passed on to future generations."[21]

By learning to live within the limits of our own ecological region, we will be able to "grow out" toward a more sustainable world. Kirkpatrick Sale identifies a number of bioregions that take both ecosystems and human communities as their base. He sees these ecosystems as the largest natural divisions since they share a common ecology, such as native vegetation and 'soil contours' that could cover thousands of square miles. Such divisions are followed by a geo-region that might be a river basin, mountain range or plateau. At the local level, which Sale calls the vita-region, is where human needs are defined. Accordingly, the vita-region must of necessity provide for the needs of its inhabitants; "this most elemental and elegant principle" of the natural world is what is called 'self-sufficiency.'

> Dwellers in the land [should] come to know the Earth, fully and honestly, the crucial and only all-encompassing task is to understand the place, the immediate specific place where we

> live [...] We must somehow live as close to it as possible, be in touch with its particular soils, its waters, its winds.[22]

The human-scale and human-centeredness to be found in Sale's thesis that each local area will sustain the basic needs of people does not logically follow. There is no apparent reason why a particular area should meet *all* basic needs. There are, after all, many large areas of the Earth where both climate and geography are not conducive to self-reliance. How are we to deal with the natural limits of an environment? Not all continents have the ecology of North America.

What is confused in bioregionalism is the tendency to equate local democracy and autonomy with a decentralisation based automatically on ecological sustainability and self-sufficiency. The application of these two principles may take different shapes in different regions depending on size. Bioregionalism assumes that local awareness of an ecosystem helps human understanding of the wider or global ecological context. There is a repetition here of the notion that the whole is the sum total of its parts common to mechanistic science. This claim is as erroneous as that held by Deep Ecology to the effect that since all things are ecologically and sub-atomically connected, our minds are also connected in a similar organic manner. This spiritual idea, "Being is knowing" is challenged by those who believe that the ecological basis of human life would need to be understood through a conscious process of learning. Knowing the specificity of one's own region would need to be mixed with a local, regional and global program for self-conscious *political* action. We need to understand the ecological reality of the Earth in a social context. Thus it appears that bioregionalism tends toward New Age cultural perspectives, rejecting social and political activism as a privileged means of effecting desired change. What is refreshing about bioregionalism is its claim that the 'natural' boundary of human social organisation need not be the nation-state, or the political borders that have been drawn within states, such as counties, cities, districts. Making the primary place of political decision-making the ecological context within which we live lends our future toward a 'natural' internationalism.

Ecofeminism

Ecofeminism has its origins in women's antimilitarism mobilisations. It was defined by the Left Green Network in their manifesto as follows:

> The liberation of women is essential to the creation of a free, peaceful, ecological society. Though capitalism has carried the dehumanization of people and the destruction of nature to new heights, the roots of our social and ecological crisis are older than capitalism. They go back thousands of years to the emergence of patriarchy, and with it, the early militarism of Neolithic warrior castes, a turn of history that laid the basis for the male-oriented culture structured around hierarchy, domination and conquest that has poisoned our social development ever since.
>
> Ecofeminism affirms the historical and life experience of women as nurturing beings with a strong sense of connection

> to nature that cultural feminism has emphasized, while refusing to accept a biological determinism that reduces the explanation of male domination to genetics. Ecofeminism also affirms the historical analysis and critique of male domination and material exploitation that socialist feminism has emphasized, while refusing to accept an anti-naturalism that seeks to build a realm of human freedom by denying our connection to nature and regarding non-human nature as existing purely for instrumental human ends. Ecofeminism seeks to draw the best insights of both cultural and socialist feminism into the non-dualistic, holistic view of society and nature (including human nature) that it is has drawn from social ecology.[23]

Since the publication of this articulation of ecofeminism by social ecologists, a variety of ecofeminist schools have emerged. Carolyn Merchant, for instance, identifies liberal ecofeminism, cultural ecofeminism, social ecofeminism, and socialist ecofeminism, all of which are variants of the initial formulation.[24]

In *Finding Our Way: Rethinking Ecofeminist Politics*, Janet Biehl critiques a kind of ecofeminism that takes its cues from an obscure spiritualism and esoteric nature nostalgia, a tendency quite present in the 1990s, rather than a coherent programme of political change.[25] To her such ecofeminism had become so heavily influenced by the irrational to the point of embracing goddess worship and witchcraft. Crystals and pentagrams, chanting and drum-beating, rituals and meditations used to raise group consciousness are considered by Janet Biehl and other political ecologists as ineffective in dealing with the ecological crisis. Further, she argues that cultural symbols should not be confused with social realities. Much of ecofeminism:

> biologize[s] and essentialize[s] the caretaking and nurturing traits [of women] and reject[s] scientific and cultural advances just because they were advocated by men.[26]

Thankfully, ecofeminism isn't as narrow as such tendencies in the 1990s which Janet Biehl critiques. In Bookchin's social ecology, feminism is completely commensurate with his critique of the development of hierarchy in early civilisations. Abdullah Oçalan, the imprisoned political and intellectual leader of the Kurdish movement whose ideas on 'democratic confederalism' are reverberating across the world, advances Bookchin's analysis to identify patriarchy as the primordial source of civilisation's social oppressions and ecological crises. In this analysis of the ancient roots of modern crises, Oçalan points to the connection between the emergence of patriarchy and hierarchy with the phenomenon of environmental exploitation. He retraces the roots of this crisis to the development of patriarchy during the period of Neolithic civilisations in Mesopotamia, when decentralised collectivist cultures were exiled by the earliest forms of hierarchy. Suddenly, egalitarian societies were then ruled by a male priest-class who claimed power by divine appointment in order to centralise the governance of agricultural, administrative, religious and eventually military matters. Spiritualities that revered the sacred Feminine were gradually expelled by theologies with male characters of power, domination and war. Production for subsistence was superseded by surplus accumulation and an overreliance on agriculture in Mesopotamia. The result was, parallel to profound social mutations, a significant rupture between humanity and the Earth which led to both social oppression and ecological exploitation.[27]

Today, patriarchy is still very much a reality as much as capitalist exploitation and ecological crisis. Indeed, on a global scale, women have been shown to be the biggest victims of poverty, colonialism and climate change. Yet beyond victimhood, empowering women at the local level has been described as one of the most powerful solutions. Today it is women, and especially indigenous and racialised women in the Global South, who are at the forefront of leadership in social and economic change through initiatives such as agroecology, micro-finance, education and community building. This is true also for radical struggles against extractivism; in North America, from Standing Rock in North Dakota to Unist'ot'en in BC to the fight against Line 9 between Sarnia and Montreal, indigenous women have been the public image and voice from the front lines of these struggles.

This ideological map of citizen responses to the environmental crisis cannot be completed without a discussion of what is arguably the most coherent and promising current within the ecology movement, political ecology, under which rubric belong the Greens in their eco-Marxist, eco-socialist, and social ecologist manifestations. It is to this task that the following section is devoted.

SECTION THREE

Political Ecology and Social Ecology

The first and most important point to be made about ecologism is that it is not the same as environmentalism. As Jonathan Porritt, Director of Friends of the Earth and a leading speaker for the Green movement in Britain has written:

> It seems quite clear that whereas a concern for the environment (a fundamental characteristic of the ideology in its own right) is an essential part of 'being green,' it is by no means the same thing as being green. The principal difference is that ecologism argues that care for the environment presupposes radical changes in our relationship with the natural world and in our mode of social and political life. Environmentalism, on the

other hand, takes a managerial approach to environmental problems, secure in the belief that these can be solved without fundamental changes in present values or patterns of production and consumption.[28]

Origins

In the 1960s, a new Left emerged which drew inspiration from a new mix of philosophical perspectives. This movement, composed primarily of young people and active on diverse political fronts, gave rise to a number of new social movements by the beginning of the 1970s. As noted earlier, these movements included the anti-war, feminist, communitarian, and ecology movements. The basic tenets of belief and methods of action that have characterised these movements up to our own day developed in a fruitful process of cross-fertilisation which transcended national boundaries. Space limitations do not permit discussion of the numerous theories and analyses of the crisis of our society or the proposed alternatives put forward by these movements. (There is already a considerable descriptive and analytical literature on the origins and nature of the new social movements.) Here, we will simply enumerate some of the principal contributions of political ecology.

Although it is critical of science as traditionally understood, political ecology does affirm that the ecological crisis can be scientifically verified. In contrast with environmentalism, however, political ecology advances the idea that the science of ecology itself cannot be divorced from and indeed implies certain political conceptions. For example, inasmuch as the ecological crisis affects the Earth as a whole isolated attempts to solve the problem cannot but fail; there must be a coordination of efforts and this on a global scale. However, political ecology privileges action at the local and regional levels against what has been called the "imperialism of the state". In Europe, the Greens advocate the creation of a continent of regions against the pre-eminence of the nation-state, and call for concrete expressions of solidarity with the peoples of the Southern hemisphere. Another theme of political ecology is the redefinition of the quality of life in opposition to the ideology of limitless growth and endless accumulation of commodities on which the existing consumer society is founded. A snapshot of a green worldview can be developed by contrasting green values and objectives with elements of the prevailing belief system.

1. Capitalist (whether state or private) industrialism.	1. An ecological framework for sustainable development.
2. Predominance of materialist values.	2. Search for spiritual values.
3. Reductionist analysis.	3. Attempt at synthesis and organic analysis.
4. A determinist view of the future.	4. Flexibility and emphasis on personal autonomy.
5. Aggressive individualism.	5. Toward a communitarian and cooperative society.
6. Anthropocentrism.	6. Biocentric humanism.
7. External motivations.	7. Personal motivation and personal growth.
8. Rationalism.	8. Reason informed by intuition.

9. Patriarchal values.	9. Feminist values.
10. Institutionalised violence.	10. Gandhian non-violence.
11. Unlimited economic growth.	11. Quality of life and balanced growth within the limits of nature.
12. Production for unrestricted trade exchange.	12. Useful production of goods and services.
13. Unequal distribution of income.	13. Equalizing revenue.
14. World "free market."	14. Local production for local needs, self-reliance.
15. Stimulating demand rather than consumer protection.	15. Voluntary simplicity.
16. Work for its own sake.	16. Work for its own pleasure.
17. Unconditional acceptance of technological development.	17. Social development of science and technology.
18. Centralisation and large scale economies.	18. Decentralisation and human scale economies.
19. Hierarchical social structure.	19. Non-hierarchical social order.
20. Dependence on experts.	20. Participation and consultation of citizens.
21. Representative democracy.	21. Direct democracy.
22. Law and order.	22. Libertarian values.
23. National sovereignty.	23. Internationalism and solidarity.
24. Domination of nature.	24. Cooperation with nature.
25. Environmentalism.	25. Ecology.

26. Management of the environment.	26. Understanding the limits of the ecosystem.
27. Nuclear power.	27. Using renewable energy sources.
28. High energy consumption.	28. Reduction of energy consumption.
29. National security and military production.	29. Disarmament and social and civilian defense.

As noted earlier, the purpose of this book is not to probe the meaning of these concepts. But it is important to note that the range of ideas illustrated in the chart above is integral to the worldview advanced by Green parties throughout the world. These ideas evolved in part as a critical response to the limited impact of environmentalism in face of the magnitude of the ecological crisis, as well as in reaction to the failure of Marxism and social democracy to transform society. In addition to introducing genuine programmatic innovations, the Green parties that emerged throughout the world in the course of the 1980s also represented a departure in political style from that of traditional political parties and, in their emphasis on grassroots democracy, have sought to nourish a new political culture.

The first Green-type political party was founded in New Zealand in 1972 under the name the 'Values Party.' In 1973, a small political party called 'The People' was founded in Britain; it later became the 'Ecology Party' and was finally renamed the 'Green Party' in 1985. Green political parties have been founded in almost all European countries and in recent years in central and eastern Europe as well. There are also Green parties in Japan and Mexico. The European parties are linked through an international coordinating body in Brussels and through the cooperation of Greens elected to the European parliament in Strasbourg. Since the Earth Summit in Rio, Green parties throughout the world have established international connections.

In Canada, there is a small national Green party, and several provincial Green parties. In the USA, The Greens (USA), once avoided focusing on national elections, though they have since fielded presidential candidates like Ralph Nader and Jill Stein. Among the Greens on this continent there are those who see the municipality and its neighbourhoods as the exclusive site of political action. They take literally the Green slogan "think globally, act locally" and view the attempt to create Green Cities as a more historically realistic and desirable project than seeking power at the national level.

In those countries that have a political system of proportional representation the Greens have succeeded in entering a national parliament; elsewhere Greens have been elected to municipal governments and various regional legislatures. It was the rise of *Die Grünen* in West Germany and the party's first parliamentary success in 1983 that brought the word 'Green' to world political attention. *Die Grünen* published a far-reaching program for change that synthesised the most original and creative ideas of the new movements of the 1960s and 1970s. They proposed an integrated approach to the current ecological, economic and political crises, which, they stressed, are inter-related and global.

The Greens are not solely concerned with the environmental crisis, although they address it with urgency. They advocate a multi-issued approach, and promote political action through independent Green parties, in close liaison with various social movements. However, the spectrum of Green views ranges from 'light Greens' (principally reformers who advocate compromise and engaging in electoralism to "get things changed") to 'dark Greens' (fundamentalists, red Greens, and anarcho-Greens who emphasise grassroots activism—combined with selective electoral participation understood primarily as educational activity—and who synthesise radical politics, feminism and anti-militarism).

One of the main weaknesses not only of the German Greens but of the majority of Green parties is that they have failed to develop a sufficiently profound critique of the limits of liberal democracy and parliamentarism. Consequently they do not possess a radical understanding of the dynamics of state political power and the present system's capacity to co-opt forces of opposition. We will return to this crucial question later on.

Toward a New Political Culture

Every nation-state has an official national culture that serves as an institutional and psychological force of integration and socialisation. It contributes to inculcating individuals with the dominant values and modes of behavior. However, these dominant values are never accepted by everyone at all times; particularly in societies where there is some degree of pluralism, alternative political cultures may emerge, germinating in the margins.

Faced with the dominant traditions, the political ecologists have made every effort to forge a new political culture. The ecologists have thus fashioned their own myths and symbols, as well as political and cultural practices—in brief, an autonomous identity. Whether this oppositional culture can withstand the pressures of cooptation remains to be seen.

The state portrays itself as *the* protector of the people. The ecologists however regard this myth as obsolete and destructive and have put forward an alternative vision. They maintain that power should reside in citizen control at the local level, and thus the region, town or village becomes the chosen locus of political action. At the same time, they see the planet as a whole, rather than the nation-state alone, as the ultimate object of social and political transformation. Hence, the dictum: "think globally, act locally." This alternative vision of political struggle is coupled with a preference for small-scale economic development, drawing on the "small is beautiful" principle, first expressed by Fritz Schumacher. Thus, ecologists resist technocratic solutions and mammoth projects. They are suspicious of anything that exceeds the human scale. The reasons for the insistent Green concern with scale have been amplified by Jonathon Porritt who writes:

> As we approach various environmental and biological constraints on growth, so we are reaching certain institutional limits imposed by the growing incompetence and declining performance of our bureaucracies. The levels of interdependence and complexity are now so great in many bureaucracies that even the ablest of decision-makers within them are quite overwhelmed. The costs of coordinating this

Political Ecology and Social Ecology

> complexity are considerable. The larger an organization or bureaucracy becomes the more rigid and inflexible is it, and so much the less scope is there for creativity and divergent thinking. Similarly, the larger it becomes, the more likely it is that standardized, depersonalized methods of operation will increase the amount of alienation people feel.[29]

Of course, as Porritt observes, the concept of the human scale is more complex than a simple allergy to bigness. Size must be considered in qualitative and not solely quantitative terms. He suggests that what is 'too big' is "whatever size it is that takes away our dignity, makes us passive recipients rather than active participants, makes us dependent rather than self-reliant, alienates us from the work we do and the people we live with."[30]

Alongside their anti-technocratic outlook the Greens express a real commitment to creating, or rather re-creating, community. In 1986, for instance, the leader of the French Greens stated: "The commune, in particular the small rural commune, is the preferred base for the kind of society we wish. It would be a serious mistake to neglect this."

Not surprisingly, the colours green and yellow are used widely in the symbolism of ecologists, the former evoking vegetation and the latter the sun. The sunflower, a popular symbol, embodies both colours and turns toward the sun, the source of renewable energy. The bicycle is another important icon as bicycle transportation is regarded as one of the means to re-humanise society.

In contradistinction with the tendencies of traditional politics, Green politics demonstrate a keen concern with personal and social ethics, although the party is by no means considered the sole arbiter of moral conduct and much weight is given to individual conscience. For their attention to ethics, the Greens are often rewarded with derision, accused of sanctimonious exhortation and failing to grasp *realpolitik*.

Eco-socialism

There are many varieties of eco-socialism, into which category fall the eco-social democrats, who seek to blend environmentalism and democratic socialism. All social democratic political parties, including the Democratic Socialists of America and the New Democratic Party in Canada, are attempting to integrate environmental concerns into their programs. However, the programs of these parties are anchored in the metaphysic of the state, and consequently they maintain that a necessary condition for environmental protection is the election of social democrats to central political power. One of the ways that they attempt to legitimise this claim and gain credibility as spokespersons for the environment is by pointing to environmental legislation that has been enacted in social-democratic countries such as Sweden. They also seek to strengthen international bodies like the United Nations, and support foreign aid for developing countries, as in the case of the North-South Commission headed by Willy Brandt (1980) and the Brundtland Report, *Our Common Future* (1987).

Included under the rubric of eco-socialism is the eco-Marxist attempt to synthesise Marxism and ecology. Remaining within a broadly conceived Marxist theoretical framework, eco-Marxists continue to focus on political economy. While taking their distance from classical Marxist theories—which assume the limitless abundance of nature, and celebrate productivism—and attempting to move beyond reductionist analyses of the primacy of the economic, the eco-Marxists are still inclined to regard change at the point of production as the motor of all social and political change.

In their analysis of the lamentable environmental record of the former state socialist bloc, the eco-Marxists ascribe the blame to Taylorism and the wholesale importation of the Fordist model of industrial organisation.

Eco-Marxists remain uncomfortable with the dominant Green accent on decentralisation and the local as the locus of political action and social development. A prominent example of eco-Marxist theorising is the American journal, *Capitalism, Nature, Socialism*, developed under the editorship of James O'Connor. In an essay entitled "Socialism and Ecology," O'Connor objects to the Green emphasis on localism, arguing that "most ecological problems and the economic problems which are both cause and effect of the ecological problems cannot be solved locally."[31] Acknowledging that centralism as traditionally conceived by the Marxist Left has failed, he calls for the sublation of centralism and localism. He suggests that the only potentially viable form of political organisation is a democratic state but he fails to offer any indications of what concrete form such a democratised state might take.

The majority of the more traditional Marxists, for their part, remain ambivalent toward environmental and ecology movements, seeing in them a tendency to divert attention from more fundamental class issues.

By far the most sophisticated and interesting group in the eco-socialist category are the European libertarian eco-socialists, among whom are the authors of the eco-socialist manifesto *Europe's Green Alternative*. They envision a continent of autonomous regions, rather than nation-states, which are economically decentralised, shaped by feminist principles and built upon social structures that are not based on the arbitrary exercise of power. They maintain that eco-socialist change cannot be brought about by the state and they advocate citizen control of the economy. Their manifesto is worth quoting from at length. In their view the ecological movement is part of a slowly rising wave of international resistance which is "gradually eroding away all authority: employers, technocracy, patriarchy, the military, political parties, the church, the state."[32]

In a section of the manifesto subtitled "Let the State Wither Away", they declare:

> Many of the problems faced by societies can only be solved if the following two conditions are fulfilled: Firstly, the vast majority of people—in theory, all of them—must have a real possibility of defining their own needs and the responses to them, and of controlling the process from beginning to end; and secondly, that the solution should be looked for at a local and regional level, firmly rooted in grassroots experience which, thanks to the democratic and critical use of new information and communications technology, would be directly linked (with no short-circuits) to global facts. A political reaction to ecological and social risks must, above all, be democratic, decentralized and participative, and as direct

as possible. The greater the awareness of the interdependence of life and ecological and social problems, the greater the need for a right to diversity.[33]

How do they conceive of decentralisation?

> Neither feudal fragmentation, nor unification at the top only; a Europe made up of regions does not only mean not creating an authoritarian super-state, but also not replacing the current EU member states by a mosaic of smaller sovereign states. Under no condition may the totally free expression and self-determination of all the federated communities, and the people who make them up, be destroyed ...

> What is required is not destruction, but construction; not to conquer the state, but to create and experiment continually with radically new political institutions. Never before has a solution of this type been put in place on such a large scale.[34]

From the chapter "What Can We Do?" we gain an idea of what the re-definition of citizenship could mean:

> Our eco-socialist project must take into account [the] contradiction between a representative state and direct democracy. To transcend it means both changing the existing state institutions and apparatus (including political parties), and at the same time increasing direct democracy at all levels, in ways as yet unimagined. Each situation will require all the issues to be set out and examined. We will fight all attempts to make politics into a profession.[35]

Concerned with the dangers of the iron rule of oligarchy, professionalisation and cooptation, they remain wary of political parties as the exclusive form of political organisation:

> As eco-socialists we want alternative, independent, green movements to grow in strength, to respond to innovation and to create as yet undiscovered types of political organizations. We, therefore, hope that the green dynamic does not get suffocated by party politics. Organising as a party is only acceptable as a temporary compromise, in order to keep one's independence and to be able to take part in political institutions. Women must have equal representation. Dissenting views must be expressed and accepted. Responsibilities must be shared, rotated and kept in check. No line, group or person must be able to impose their will over all others; however, individuality must not drown in mediocrity and stereotypes.[36]

In many of their declarations and proposals these libertarian eco-socialists display an affinity with the current of thought known as social ecology, which we discuss below. They stop short, however, of embracing the municipalist approach to ecological and social change integral to the school of social ecology. Although the libertarian eco-socialists in Europe reject the nation-state in favor of a continent of regions, they fail to identify a specific configuration of political and economic institutions as the potential foundation for the radical social and political changes they set as their goal.

Social Ecology

Social ecology is rooted in a rich philosophical framework that is reflected in its politics. Comprehensive and systematic, it represents the greatest advance in twentieth century eco-philosophy. The progenitor of the theory of social ecology is the American radical ecologist Murray Bookchin. Since the 1950s, he laboured brilliantly to lay the foundation of this philosophy in which history, technology and urbanism are interwoven. Bookchin was no academic philosopher ensconced in some university. Rather, he was a radical scholar who, in addition to being a prolific writer, was a political activist over many decades, and he constantly sought new ways of generating civic politics while remaining resolutely anti-capitalist and anti-statist.

His most important philosophical work was *The Ecology of Freedom* (1982) and his most important political work was *Urbanization without Cities* (1987). In these and other works, social ecology is described as "social" in its fundamental recognition that nearly all present ecological problems, indeed the environmental crisis as such, arise from deep-seated social problems; there can be no separation of the 'ecological question' from the 'social question'. Thus, our environmental problems cannot be clearly understood, much less resolved, without resolutely dealing with the concrete social problems within society. To make this point very real: the exploitation of the natural world is a reflection of the exploitation and hierarchical domination that occurs between people; humanity's troubled relationship with nature is a symptom of the socio-economic, ethnic, gender and cultural conflicts and alienations that exist within our societies. These social disharmonies are economically manifested in trade centered on profit, the exploitation of workers, out-of-control urbanisation, industrial expansion, large-scale mining, and the identification of progress with corporate self-interest among many other phenomena. Such features of the system are only further compounded by cultures of vulgar materialism and pathological consumption and the plethora of attendant social consequences. Thus, such social dislocations are reproduced in all the most serious ecological dislocations we face today—apart, to be sure, from those that are produced by natural disasters.

To separate the ecological crisis from the social crisis—or to give only token recognition of their crucial relationship—would be to grossly misconstrue the sources of the growing environmental crisis. Unless we realise that the present society is anchored in market capitalism, that it is structured around the brutally competitive imperative of growth for the sake of growth, and that it is a thoroughly impersonal, self-operating mechanism—all of which needs to be replaced—we will grope for answers elsewhere, falsely blaming perceived enemies for our environmental impasse, such as technology, immigration or population growth. In short, we will tend to focus on the symptoms of a grim social pathology rather than on the pathology itself, while our efforts will be directed toward limited goals whose attainment is more cosmetic than curative. Further, we will fail to see that a mentality rooted in domination and exploitation, and the exploitative class relationships that ensue, thoroughly permeate and deform us and our society. Only an understanding with such a scope will

Political Ecology and Social Ecology

help explain why and how the natural world is dominated and exploited by our civilisation. It is in this way social ecologists openly admit the ugly truth of the problem and the scale of the project required to transforming it.

The deep systemic vision and politics of this radical ecology stands in contrast to the reformism dominating mainstream environmentalism, exemplified by the NGOs and their failure to confront the nature of corporate power, its hold on the economy and its dominant influence over popular culture. They also fail to challenge the stultifying grip of conventional politics over much of society's political culture, the consequent insularity of the vast majority of politicians and their hir s, and especially the disconnectedness of the people from the ruling political institutions; in addition to this is the question of the mass media and its role in manipulating public opinion and manufacturing consent. Indeed, one can say that, in failing to seriously confront such structural political issues, much of this moderate environmentalism generates a false consciousness, often directing the anger of concerned people merely into harmless exercises like writing letters or donating money toward campaigns, and this for issues which, albeit urgent, are peripheral to the systemic problem of capitalism itself. This is simply inadequate, as much as such organisations may seem to be active.

In Canada, an embodiment of this situation of deliberate ambiguity is the important but limited contribution of David Suzuki who, despite his champion role in public education of the environmental crisis, skirts around the question of system change. Then there is the contribution of Naomi Klein who, in her most recent book *This Changes Everything*, successfully analyzes the central role of free market neoliberal capitalism as causing the climate crisis but shies away from any road map toward a radical politics that could transcend such a system. With the reformist environmentalism of such public spokespeople, widely covered by the media, there is an enforcement of the unimpressively feeble role of environmentalism.

Wishy-washy environmentalism also manifests itself in other senses that distract the environmental movement. The effort of some environmentalists, while posing as political actors, to give priority to a sentimentally pantheistic 'eco-spirituality' over the need to address social factors raises serious questions about their ability to deal with reality. Nor need we be distracted by 'lifestyle activism' which clings to image and sociability, exhibiting their political tendencies as a kind of fashion, and so confusing this kind of sub-culture with genuine radical community (the latter of which will be seriously discussed in a moment). And of course there is the widespread trend of eco-consumerism where marketing and PR industries promote the cult of the consumer as the agent of ecological change. As tough and disagreeable as it might seem, we must face the fact that economic growth for its own sake—to which corporate, state and bureaucratic interests are duly obedient—is much more capable of shaping the future of the natural world than is privatistic spiritual self-generation, 'radical' subculture or individualistic consumption. The massive systems of domination must be confronted by collective action, and on a huge scale, by a major social movement that challenges the sources of the crisis—the social forces and the resulting economic structures.

The Praxis of Social Ecology

Bookchin elaborated a philosophy of dialectical naturalism which understands society and ecology as interconnected; its sweeping analysis traces the contours of natural and social evolution to the historical emergence and development of hierarchy, exploitation and domination which he claims are the roots of contemporary social and ecological problems. It is in this way that a non-dualistic conception of the relations between human society and nature that could provide the basis for a "genuinely objective ethics." "It is eminently *natural*," he writes, "for humanity to create a second nature from its evolution in first nature."[37] This second nature, Bookchin explains, consists in "humanity's development of a uniquely human culture, a wide variety of institutionalised human communities, an effective human technics, a richly symbolic language, and a carefully managed source of nutriment." This is not imposed on biological first nature, but a result of first nature's own evolutionary processes. Thus, first and second nature do not exist in isolation from one another but in a mutually enriching organic relation and in which biological reality is reworked in a dialectical process into social reality. The problem, as he sees it, is that social evolution began in the course of human history to assume a distorted character, moving away from organic cooperative forms of social organisation. What is required in the face of the ecological crisis is not a (in any case impossible) return to primitivism but a radical integration of nature and society on the basis of the development of eco-communities.

On top of such analysis, he defined 'politics' far more comprehensively than its generally received meaning as 'statecraft.' In particular, in "The Creation of Politics," Chapter 3 in *Urbanization without Cities*, Bookchin extrapolates on Aristotle to show that politics is inherent to human nature and that this is most embodied through the active engagement in the everyday affairs of our immediate community. Social ecologists see in these ideas the basis of a new politics, a politics that eschews reliance on the state in favor of the empowerment of communities. Enter Bookchin's notion of 'Libertarian Municipalism': in social ecology the municipality is theorised as the natural locus of social, political and environmental change and the neighbourhood, city or town, are conceived as the base for a new democratic politics. As Bookchin explains:

> The municipality … is the most immediate political arena of the individual, the world that is literally a doorstep beyond the privacy of the family and the intimacy of personal friendships. In that primary political arena, where politics should be conceived in the Hellenic sense of literally managing the polis or community, the individual can be transformed from a mere person into an active citizen, from a private being into a public being. Given this crucial arena that literally renders the citizen a functional being who can participate directly in the future of society, we are dealing with a level of human interaction that is more basic (apart from the family itself) than any level that is expressed in representative forms of governance, where collective power is literally transmuted into power embodied by one or a few individuals. The municipality is thus the most authentic arena of public life, however much it may have been distorted over the course of history.[38]

This is reflected in the commitment of political ecologists or the Greens to decentralisation, self-reliance and localism. Unlike eco-socialism even of the libertarian variety, social ecology spells out and grounds an effective and comprehensive alternative form of administration that challenges the central state in every way. The social ecologists are in fact the only Greens who fill this theoretical lacuna.

Conceiving the municipality as "the most authentic arena of public life," it follows for social ecologists that Green electoral activity should be confined to participation in municipal elections rather than aspiring to so-called 'higher levels of government'. As Bookchin suggests, it is qualitatively different for Greens to run a candidate for mayor on a libertarian municipalist platform than for them to participate in elections at other levels of government even as a forum in which to advance libertarian municipalist ideas. One cannot, he argues, divorce the office from its context and make an abstraction of it. The powers of a mayor are substantively different from the powers of, say, a state governor or a provincial premier; they are subject to greater public scrutiny and control, being closer to the people.[39]

Confined to the municipal level, electoral participation must involve promoting a radical program for the decentralisation of power from the 'higher levels' of the central state to the municipality, and, further, from the central city council to the neighbourhoods. The social ecologists privilege, as a political strategy, the creation of neighbourhood councils or assemblies, the forms of which depend on the size of the city. The process of municipal decentralisation would not only re-structure city council to create an assembly of mandated and revocable delegates from the neighbourhood councils; the office of the mayor would itself be rendered a largely symbolic position.

Thus, although sanctioning a limited form of electoral participation, social ecologists remain critics of the existing system of parliamentary democracy. They have drawn the negative lessons of the long and unsuccessful history of socialist attempts to use the parliamentary system to their own ends, attempts which have usually ended in their becoming caught up in the narrow logic of the parliamentary process and in the neutering of radical political programs. For this reason both the New Left and the Greens have tried to enrich existing political democracy with extra-parliamentary action and organisation, although it is not clear that this commitment immunises them from the co-optive pressures of traditional politics.

Social ecology introduces, as a programmatic idea, the creation of dual power in which official political power is sought but only simultaneously with the creation of decentralised bases of popular control. The strategy is to devolve ever more power to the base in a gradual process of dismantling the central state. Of all the perspectives on power articulated by political ecologists, the social ecologist insistence on dual power is the one which is best grounded historically and philosophically, and thus the most realistic strategy. Yet, unlike many programs of political change trumpeted by the Old Left, this is not something abstract or mechanically 'scientific' but fundamentally involves a particularly subjective social form: community.

The Real Meaning of Community

We have here encountered much mention of community as a vehicle for the urgent social change needed to challenge the serious crises our civilisation faces. But what is meant by a concept that could seem so nebulous and clichéd? Insincerely invoked by media and politicians, the use of the term 'community' has been so mangled and hackneyed in recent times that it is in danger of being hollowed out of meaning altogether. It is currently loosely (mis-)used to describe all manner of human interactions, such as a 'sporting community' or a 'virtual community', descriptors which refer instead to associations or networks or affiliations; but beyond such debilitating and perniciously corrosive misuse of the word is a concept fundamental to our social existence that bears considerable weight in an imagination of social change.

Coming to a clear and precise definition of community is crucial, and even more so in the megalopolis where "all that is solid melts into air", where facts of social structures once deemed immutable have been significantly transformed or even lost. The creation—or reclamation—of community may be a complex and multi-layered process but one thing is clear: it is critically predicated on the idea of place. This is the neighbourhood, the basic building block of the town and city. At least for social ecology, a sense and reality of community forms out of spatial, on-the-ground bases, a geographical area in which a number of people have made a long-term commitment to its health and flourishing and which has the politics of social change. A community should have an economic, social and political identity and be a power base for political outreach beyond the locality and into the city as a whole (an excellent example of which will be explored in the next section). A commitment to such a definition is the first step on the road to self-sufficient, self-managing, self-designing communities. The second, as discussed earlier, is nurturing a fabric of counter-institutions as a dual power involving grassroots democratic neighbourhood councils or assemblies.

In addition to community, the further ingredients include decentralisation, localism, self-sufficiency, and confederation—all of which cannot be understood as separate but rather are equally viable options; they are inextricably related in the vision of ecological interdependence advanced in the theory of libertarian or confederal municipalism. As Bookchin writes:

> To be sure, without the institutional structures that cluster around our use of these terms and without taking them in combination with each other, we cannot hope to achieve a free ecologically oriented society … Decentralism and self-sustainability must involve a much broader principle of social organization than mere localism. Together with decentralization, approximations to self-sufficiency, humanly scaled communities, eco-technologies, and the like, there is a compelling need for democratic and truly communitarian forms of inter-dependence—in short, for libertarian forms of confederalism … What, then, is confederalism? It is above all a network of administrative councils whose members or delegates are elected from popular face-to-face democratic assemblies, in the various villages, towns, and even neighborhoods of large cities. The members of these confederal councils are strictly mandated, recallable, and responsible to the

assemblies that choose them for the purpose of coordinating and administering the policies formulated by the assemblies themselves. Their function is thus a purely administrative and practical one, not a policy-making one like the function of representatives in republican systems of government.[40]

And he continues:

Confederalism is thus a way of perpetuating the interdependence that should exist among communities and regions—indeed, it is a way of democratising that interdependence without surrendering the principle of local control. While a reasonable measure of self-sufficiency is desirable for every locality and region, confederalism is a means for avoiding local parochialism on the one hand and an extravagant national and global division of labor on the other. In short, it is a way in which a community can retain its identity and roundedness while participating in a sharing way with the larger whole that makes up a balanced ecological society …

Confederalism as a principle of social organization reaches its fullest development when the economy itself is confederalized by placing local farms, factories, and other needed enterprises in local municipal hands—that is, when a community, however larger or small, begins to manage its own economic resources in an interlinked network with other communities.[41]

The pedigree of this new democratic politics can be traced back to Peter Kropotkin's 'Commune of Communes', Martin Huber's 'Community of Communities' and the reflections of Paul Goodman. However, social ecology has given the concept of direct democracy an ecological, geographic, and political-economic spatial dimension that can serve as the building blocks for a new society. It proposes that the way to save our society, and with it human civilisation, is to radically transform it by replacing domination, hierarchy and exploitation with a socially and ecologically harmonious society. This necessitates a richly textured confederation of eco-communities deploying eco-technologies in the quest to restore a balance between humans and nature. The objective of superseding hierarchy presupposes, of course, the systematic extirpation of racism, class society, and the inequality between women and men. In a word, unless society and its major institutions of power are fundamentally changed, we cannot hope to establish that balance with nature that will permit us to reverse the crisis.

It is a fact that, in many cities, elementary notions of participatory democracy are sought, instinctively almost, by everyday citizens. Citizen initiatives could be welded together in coalitions as the basis of a cohesive 'Right to the City' movement (more on this later). In this rich soil, where some sense of community exists or can be cultivated, the implementation of a social ecology-inspired strategy can be promising and crucial.

It is a hopeful sign that social ecology has been gaining ground in the larger ecological movement, renewing the legacy bequeathed by libertarian socialism and anarchism. It is hoped that confederal municipalist Green political organisations are organised, wherever possible, with a social ecology-informed program, setting in motion the dynamic of dual power.

SECTION FOUR

A Road Map Beyond Mere Environmentalism

Looking around us almost daily there is growing evidence of the environmental crisis and the particular role of cities in this. Since 2007, over half of humanity—3.5 billion people—now live in cities. This is a major shift of historic dimensions, and full of implications for social transformation. By 2055, an estimated 75% of the world's population will be living in urban areas. Urbanisation is galloping in growth across the planet. As never before, the migration of the poor and the destitute is on a massive scale as they leave the countryside to seek out imagined greener pastures in the great cities. All this and more are putting enormous pressure on such cities, in both northern and southern hemispheres, who can now hardly cope with any number of serious problems; hovering over it all is the question as to what the near future holds.

Cities today occupy only 2 per cent of the Earth's land, but account for over 70 per cent of energy consumption and as much as 70 per cent of global greenhouse gas emissions. These UN statistics have terribly important consequences for humanity. Cities are, and will continue to be, at the nexus of global crises related to economic recession, energy insecurity, water scarcity or flooding, high food prices, vulnerability to climate change and natural disasters.

Cities, consistently undermined by national governments, have been underfunded and underrepresented in the upper circles of the power elite that determine 'national priorities.' The result is cities, big and small, have serious problems of political legitimacy; weakened, they face large-scale disinterest by citizens. Moreover, the sense of community is being hollowed out of neighbourhoods as the city experiences large-scale urbanisation. Due to these factors, cities on the whole do not have the will to transform themselves into the democratic arenas for citizen participation in decision-making that they could be.

And this in spite of the looming issues of urban management. Collapsing infrastructure is a major issue, as is inefficient public transit, water security, waste management, energy and fuel waste, overflowing landfills, flooding, and water and air pollution, all with serious effects on public health. Capitalist urbanisation, whether state-sponsored or corporate-driven, simply cannot handle the urban crisis, substantially aggravating the environmental crisis. Cities appear locked into unsustainable models of urbanisation.

The other side of the economic coin is that as cities develop a critical bearing on the future of the planet, those of the world's emerging economies are becoming the drivers of the global economy while the planet's resources are rapidly being depleted. So the environmental cannibalism of the large cities of the North is only accentuated by the rampant urban sprawl, the degradation of the environment and the proliferation of slums in the cities of the South.

Over and above the very heavy footprint on the Earth's environment that is the current lot of cities and urbanisation, the economic place of cities in the world economy must be taken into account. Jane Jacobs was amongst the first to research and demonstrate that it is urban areas that drive and in fact dominate the national economies. She showed that 'national economies' are largely mythical constructions, and that it is more urban based regional economies that represent the real economic driving forces in society. Saskia Sassen has taken this thesis even further with her research which demonstrates that, today, 'global cities' are in fact the dominant conduits through which the transnational corporations determine the rise and decline of the world economy. Indeed, the consequence of this is clearly demonstrated in the dramatic social revolts, centered in cities, which erupt in response to international crises in capitalism, especially around the 2008-2009 meltdown of market and finance capitalism.

David Harvey, in his numerous books, places the city at the heart of capital accumulation and class struggles. Cities are central to struggles over capital and they are the frontline for strategies seeking to control access to urban resources which dictate the quality and organisation of daily life. His basic thesis is supported by considerable historical evidence and contemporary analysis. Harvey notes:

> Conventional economics routinely treats investment in the built environment in general, and in housing in particular, along with urbanization, as some mere side-bar to the more important affairs that go on in some fictional entity called 'the national economy.' The sub-field of 'urban economics' is thus the area where inferior economists go while the big guns ply their macroeconomic trading skills elsewhere.[42]

In his recent book, *Rebel Cities: From the Right to the City to the Urban Revolution*, Harvey, an urban geographer with a libertarian Marxist perspective, provides historical coverage of the idea of the 'The Right to the City' thesis from its origins with the French theorist Henri Lefebvre to the field of political economy (more on The Right to the City later). He then singles out 'rebel cities' that reclaim the city as a site of anti-capitalist struggle, noting:

> The history of urban-based class struggles is stunning. The successive revolutionary movements in Paris from 1789 through 1830 and 1848 to the Commune of 1871 constitute the most obvious nineteenth century example. Later events include the Petrograd Soviet, the Shanghai Communes of 1927 and 1967, the Seattle General Strike of 1919, the role of Barcelona in the Spanish Civil War, the uprising in Cordoba in 1969, and the more general urban uprisings in the United States in the 1960s, the urban-based movements of 1968 (Paris, Chicago, Mexico

City, Bangkok, and others, including the so-called 'Prague Spring,' and the rise of neighborhood associations in Madrid that fronted the anti-Franco movement in Spain around the same time). And in more recent times we have witnessed echoes of these older struggles in the Seattle anti-globalization protests of 1999 (followed by similar protests in Quebec City, Genoa, and many other cities as part of a widespread alternative globalization movement). More recently we have seen mass protests in Tahrir Square in Cairo, in Madison, Wisconsin, in the Plaza del Sol in Madrid and Catalunya in Barcelona, and in Syntagma Square in Athens as well as revolutionary movements and rebellions in Oaxaca in Mexico, in Cochabamba (2000 and 2007) and El Alto (2003 and 2005) in Bolivia along with very different but equally important political eruptions in Buenos Aires in 2001–02, and in Santiago in Chile (2006 and 2011).[43]

It should be noted that Harvey sympathetically acknowledges the analysis and insights of Murray Bookchin.

Space limitations do not permit here a detailed presentation of the economics of urbanisation and the central role of cities in the world economy. Suffice it to note that the two are related.

The 'Global Cities Index,' an important tool in economic analysis, lists 66 global cities which drive the world economy. The paucity of actions to deal with the world-wide environmental crisis shown by national governments at the recent Rio+20 summit forced even former UN Secretary General, Ban Ki-moon, to declare that "our struggle for global sustainability will be won or lost in cities," a statement echoed by Al Gore at the end of his documentary, *An Inconvenient*

Truth. For the first time, the term 'governmental stakeholders,' when referring to local and sub-national governments, is being used in the UN. There is even talk of revising the UN Charter to institute a Local Government Chamber to the UN General Assembly, a potentially significant development beyond the obsolete and undemocratic centrality of states in the UN. The Council of Europe already maintains a Congress of European Municipalities and Regions, and the European Union maintains a Committee of Regions. These are some indicators that the power elites are being forced to adjust their understanding of the huge historic changes taking place.

Sadly the political implications of the analysis outlined above, with which radical social change can be given priority, are side-tracked by the established orthodoxy of the Left. The city as a geopolitical terrain for the challenging of global capitalism and the state seems to have passed by most of the Left including the anarchists. This Left is invited to consider the reflection of urban sociologist Robert Park, a passage also used by Harvey:

> The city is man's most consistent and, on the whole, his most successful attempt to remake the world he lives in more after his heart's desire. The city is the world which man created; it is the world in which he is therefore condemned to live. Thus indirectly, without a clear sense of the nature of his task, in remaking the city man has remade himself.[44]

Theory without practice is aimless. So following are two real world examples directly inspired by the ideas of social ecology. The first example is in an advanced capitalist society, and the second example is in a society struggling to be reborn in the so-called Middle East.

The Case of Montreal

The sensibility that social ecology reflects arose alongside community organising and the notions of participatory democracy advocated and practiced by the New Left in Montreal in the 1960s. The practice of community organising arose with the self-organisation of the poor and underclass as a means to empower the powerless in society. There were parallel movements among both Anglophones and Francophones. There was much political work done to build tenant rights organisations, social housing campaigns (decent housing was advocated as a right for the first time), and anti-poverty coalition building, all with an anti-capitalist and anti-authoritarian edge. This daily work was done alongside a radical student movement involved in anti-war work on the one hand while practicing student syndicalism (a form of trade unionism) on the other. The trade union movement was also turned on its head when one of the major federations began to advocate a 'second front.' That is, a front which advocated the establishment of a terrain on which unionised workers and others acted beyond the workplace, placing themselves in their neighbourhoods alongside other community active citizens.

For over a decade and a half, the political culture of Montreal was seeded with the most radical ideas with which thousands identified. The modern anarchists of Montreal arose in the late 1960s around the ideas of Paul Goodman and

Murray Bookchin who came to the city both as educational public speakers but also in organising numerous active affinity groups. In one particular downtown neighbourhood, called Milton-Parc, those affinity groups gathering around Bookchin's social ecology played a determining role in the destiny of this neighbourhood. This community become involved in what has been described as "the biggest citizen versus developer confrontation in Canada," gaining victory to form the biggest non-profit cooperative housing project in North America based on a community land trust.

The story begins in the early 1960s when a real estate company quietly bought up a large six block area with the objective of demolishing everything and building an upper class set of apartments and commercial skyscrapers. The company publicly announced its demolition and construction plans in 1968. From that year onward, a broad-based militant urban struggle began in the downtown neighbourhood of Milton-Parc which lasted some eleven years. It ranged from door knocking to demonstrations, petitions, occupations, squatting and non-violent direct action; a sit-in at the offices of the real estate company led to arrests, jail and a trial by jury where the 59 arrested were found not guilty of public mischief (an accusation with a potential five year jail term).

The consequence of this base-building and much other organising work that followed resulted in establishing the Milton-Parc non-profit social housing project for low-income citizens. The community land trust denies market capitalism a prime six city block area in the downtown of the city from all land speculation. Imagine an entire neighbourhood where the buying and selling of property is not permitted. As an urban land trust, it is the largest in North America. Such an accomplishment has become a source of inspiration, recognised nationally in a postage stamp by Canada Post and internationally as a winner in World Habitat Awards.

What ensued was a process of social reconstruction of the houses that were in poor condition; once they were fully renovated to the best of housing standards, the community set up 22 self-managed non-profit housing coops and non-profit housing associations, all confederated together, beginning in the late 1970s into the 1980s, all of which continues to exist today. The project involves over a thousand people in 642 housing units of various sizes and eleven small businesses. This community based neighbourhood project practices democratic self-management and cooperates with other city-wide organisations; many of the prominent individuals involved were inspired by the sentiments of social ecology.

In 1996, the community-based libertarians then established the city's first social ecology institution, the Urban Ecology Centre of Montreal. Its mandate was to focus on all the major issues of the urban question through the lens of social ecology. It is today a major social actor in the larger Montreal region having organised five citizen summits, each one larger in number than the preceding one, which gathered diverse Montreal citizen movements in a spirit informed by the World Social Forum; the networking involved hundreds of citizens in a variety of social actions across the city. The idea of a Montreal Charter of Rights and Responsibilities for citizens and the further idea of participatory budgeting emerged from these summits. The impact of these citizen summits, along with the evolution of the political culture since the 1960s, is to be seen abundantly in the urban neighbourhoods of Montreal. Participatory democracy has become a part of neighbourhood political culture and is often practiced as the social reconstruction of society is advocated by citizens active in community affairs and in community organisations.

Other neighbourhoods also continued the practice of the 60s politics of community organisation so that Montreal has a very important civil society of all colours which undertakes important defensive campaigns against urban deterioration with a pronounced commitment to democracy. The politically active neighbourhood of Pointe St. Charles is another more recent pole of grassroots activity and movement building where citizen activists are strongly influenced by social ecology. In 2006, a major casino which was to be built in the heart of the Point St. Charles area was successfully blocked by vigorous community action. Furthermore, this area is home to the last of Montreal's community-controlled medical clinics and the recurring threats to it have been consistently fended off.

Since the beginning of the 21st century, all this community organising has had an impact on the municipal government. A number of democratic reforms have resulted, leaving openings which have been occupied by civil society. A significant re-definition of citizenship is clear in how many citizens consider themselves primarily citizens of Montreal more than citizens of a nation or province. The envelope of democracy is constantly enlarged with citizens initiating public policy instead of simply lobbying politicians. The whole idea of political intermediaries is challenged as the seeds of direct democracy start sprouting.

A product of the Montreal Charter mentioned above, the 'Right to Initiative', allows Montrealers to initiate public policy debates and consultations through the Office de consultation publique de Montréal (OCPM) on a wide range of important issues. One is example is that, several years ago, more than 29,800 citizens (far beyond the quota of 15,000) signed a petition demanding participation in public policy decision-making on the issue of urban agriculture. The politicians therefore must change course on this or that given topic in between elections. Thus, a political electric current is visibly transmitted, and Montrealers are exercising a right which does not exist elsewhere in North America at the urban level. The public desire to have citizens involved in economic decision-making and participatory budgeting is a movement toward economic democracy that has been added to the popular mix. People's impatience with the status quo and the political and economic establishment is clearly in evidence. During the spring of 2015, another citizen's initiative was launched, collecting signatures for a public consultation on the dependence of the city on fossil fuels, to which the City immediately responded by granting a public hearing.

The spirit of direct democracy was powerfully and famously manifested in Montreal during the Quebec mass student strike in the spring and summer of 2012. In response to dramatic tuition hikes planned by the neo-liberal Charest provincial government, protests erupted, with students striking for half of the year. A deep desire for fundamental change burst forth, shaping the practice of direct democracy in student assemblies. Significantly, the striking students reached out beyond the student movement; every evening, students would march into the neighbourhoods of Montreal, welcomed by the clamor of residents standing in front of their homes and banging pots in solidarity. In fact, later in the uprising, the student movement began to embrace broader social, economic and political demands, even being joined by a social strike that would include non-student workers. The student strike was successful, capsizing the government and reversing the tuition hikes, a powerful example of the force of experimenting in such new politics.

Rojava: Social Ecology in Syrian Kurdistan

History has several examples of the impact of grassroots community based organising that show the why and how that such practices can work. From the Popular Assemblies that formed the backbone of the second French Revolution of 1792, to soviets that sprung up during the 1917 upheavals in Russia. Such deliberative councils have emerged from time to time as they did recently in Argentina and Spain and elsewhere.

Currently, in the Middle East, the left-wing Kurdish movement in Syrian and Turkish Kurdistan have turned to the ideas of social ecology. They have even recently implemented a version of this to form an autonomous political system in Rojava, a region of three cantons in the north-eastern corner of Syria along the Turkish border. There, the citizens are seeking to rebuild an economy based on cooperatives and democratic citizen control, initiating what is in effect a social revolution.

Grassroots economic and socio-political decision-making is made based at the community level through face-to-face assemblies, deliberating upon all the various issues that the communities face; these assemblies then send democratically accountable representatives through successive councils that operate at the neighbourhood, city and regional levels, thus scaling up this project of grassroots democracy to an expansive yet decentralised network of mutual aid.

They have also developed a multifaceted radical feminist program, reflecting gender equality throughout this society. Currently, a strictly enforced policy of affirmative action ensures gender parity in all levels of representation from Party Presidency to neighbourhood councils through the co-chair principle. This contributes to how the women's movement is autonomously organised socially, politically and militarily.[45]

In addition, ethnic tolerance toward all people from various ethnic groups and religions is a basic right in practice, extending to non-Kurdish/non-Muslim minorities such as Arabs, Christians, Yezidis, Assyrians, Zoroastrians, Armenians and Turkmen; secularism at official levels and respect of all minorities is widely insisted upon and respected.

An interesting paradox is the fact that these left-wing Kurds, formerly grouped around the national liberation political party, the PKK, have abandoned their once stringently adhered to dogmatic Marxism-Leninism in favor of much of social ecology; this is due, in part, to their leader, Abdullah Öcalan, reading Bookchin's ideas while in a Turkish prison. For example, Öcalan directly borrows from Bookchin by touting 'democratic confederalism' as the democratic and feminist alternative to the rule of the nation-state and the capitalist system.[46]

Such a remarkable social-political project has come under serious threat. Kobani, a key border town in Rojava between Syria and Turkey, has been the target of several intense assaults by ISIS due to its strategic location and yet has been heroically defended by the YPG and YPJ, the People's Defense Units, democratically-controlled volunteer-run militias. Though the infrastructure of Kobani has been largely destroyed in such assaults and though the city is almost deserted, the residents are engaged in the city's reconstruction even enduring ongoing ISIS attacks. Furthermore, the Turkish government has maintained a closed border policy, preventing support from Kurdish allies in Turkey; indeed, in mid-2015, the Turkish president, Recep Tayyip Erdoğan, even threatened to invade Rojava to crush Kurdish autonomy.

No doubt there are flaws and contradictions in such a region which is effectively a war zone. But it is a fact that this grassroots strategy has proven far more effective in the brief period following its adoption in 2005 than almost anything promoted by the Western environmentalists and most others on the Left. The key to Rojava's survival, in spite of three years of civil war and an international embargo, is being based in communities actively participating in this democratic project. Suffice it to say, a book that has been widely consulted upon by leaders in these councils, including Öcalan himself, is Murray Bookchin's *Urbanization without Cities*, which includes a chapter entitled "The Meaning of Confederalism."

The Right to the City

In 1968, in the heat of the biggest general strike in history when 10 million people were on strike in France, Henri Lefebvre published his *Le Droit à la Ville* (The Right to the City) wherein he articulated a profound analysis of urban space and proposed a radical theory whereby a transformation can take place. David Harvey sums it up thus:

> The Right to the City is far more than the individual liberty to access urban resources, it is a right to change ourselves by changing the city. It is, moreover, a common rather than an individual right since this transformation inevitably depends upon the exercise of a collective power to reshape the processes of urbanization. The freedom to make and remake our cities and ourselves is, I want to argue, one of the most precious yet most neglected of our human rights.[47]

There is to be sure, as in all movements, a political/ideological spectrum that can be seen to speak and act in the name of the Right to the City. In 2001, Brazil for example, the City Statute adopted the Right to the City into federal law. However, the real movement of the Right to the City occurs not at the institutional level but in the number of popular movements. In Latin American, Asia, South Africa, the USA, Germany and beyond, such movements bring together tenants, refugees, workers, youth, women, artists, planners, urban farmers, shack dwellers and networks of squatters which have incorporated the Right to the City idea in their struggles.

Since 2001, when the first World Social Forum (WSF) met in Porto Alegre in southern Brazil, the need to counter the dominant forces and trends that are deforming cities became very evident. From the start, the WSF represented a democratic venue which linked the local with the regional and the global and back to the local, bringing thousands upon thousands of activists from across the planet to debate, network, and form cross border working relations; such a phenomenon threw a strong light on cities, in the full sense. Such a process has favoured the emergence of urban struggles that remain, until recently, fragmented and incapable of producing transformative changes in the current urban form. Since July 2004, however, in the city of Quito, a draft of a World Charter for the Right to the City was in the making as well as an action plan, work which has been further expanded and elaborated in the following years.

The scope of the World Charter for the Right to the City, listed in part below, shows the rich scope of this programmatic perspective. The general provisions include a series of principles and strategic short-term foundations, such as:

- The full exercise of citizenship and democratic management of the city;
- The social function of the city and of urban property;
- The right to full equality without discrimination;
- The special protection of groups and persons in vulnerable situations;
- The social commitment of the private sector;
- The promotion of the solidarity economy and progressive taxation policies;

Further, under rights relative to the exercise of citizenship and to the participation in the planning, production and management of the city:

- The social production of habitat;
- Equitable and sustainable urban development;
- The right to public information;
- The right to freedom and integrity;
- The right to political participation;
- The right to associate, gather, manifest, and to the democratic use of urban public space;
- The right to justice;
- The right to public security and peaceful, supportive and multicultural coexistence;

Further, under rights to economic, social, cultural and environmental development of the city;

- The right to water and to the access and supply of domestic and urban public services;
- The right to public transportation and urban mobility;
- The right to housing;
- The right to work;
- The right to a healthy and sustainable environment.

The Charter ends with final provisions with measures for the implementation and monitoring of the Right to the City. The complete text and the action plan are available online.[48]

In addition, an international federation of cities, the United Cities and Local Government (UCLG), organised in 2010 the first World Summit on the Right to the City and in 2012 published and widely circulated the remarkable *Global Charter: Agenda for Human Rights in the City* which has been signed by a number of cities, with many others considering to sign it.[49]

The intervention of social ecologists should be especially focused on the urban question to help broaden the reflection beyond the immediate neighbourhood and to think and act on the city as a whole. Consideration should be given to what Murray Bookchin named libertarian municipalism or 'communalism': local communities organising direct democracy to take back power over their neighbourhoods, and often intervening in local elections. This can quickly proceed to a broader project of decentralising the entire urban region toward neighbourhood assemblies or councils which, together, work to establish a new political culture.

Such a new radical politics would put priority emphasis on human rights across the board, assuring gender, racial and religious equality along with establishing a genuine egalitarian rapport between youth and the older generations with vigorous action plans implementing such rights. It would broadly introduce various forms of economic democracy in the urban economy. Such measures and the many political possibilities imagined by social ecology are well outlined in Bookchin's *Urbanization without Cities*, specifically in the chapter "Toward a New Municipal Agenda." This approach can become the basis for ending the urban war against surrounding ecosystems and the war on society.[50]

SECTION FIVE

The New Politics of Social Ecology

Since the first edition of this book in 1993, what has been plainly demonstrated with innumerable cases is that the state management of the environmental crisis has been a failure resulting in the most serious consequences. Despite many international meetings, dealing with every subject from biodiversity to climate change, the national political elites have found it impossible to come to meaningful agreements to deal with the environmental crisis. Furthermore, those political elites within those countries which are most responsible for the deterioration of nature have been relatively ineffective in protecting the environment within their respective national borders.

As discussed in Section Two of this book, in 1972 researchers from the Club of Rome confronted the world with the *Limits to Growth* report. The researchers involved made the explosive prediction that, if trends continued, our civilisation would collapse during the middle of the 21st century. The task accomplished was very ambitious. The research team tracked industrialisation, population, food, use of resources, and pollution and, using computational models, a series of scenarios were plotted out to the year 2100. Assuming that we did not take serious action to reverse the prevailing practices, the researchers predicted "overshoot and collapse" in the environment, economy and population before 2070. The book's main point was that our planet is finite and the quest for unlimited growth in material products, population and so on would eventually lead to a crash. When first published, given its radical projections, such a report was not taken seriously and was instead vigorously criticised and dismissed as doomsday fantasy. However, it is now over four decades later and studies done in the last decade, such as by the Australian CSIRO, have largely vindicated the projections of the report.[51]

Indeed, halfway through 2015, alone, the republication of this book has been surrounded by a string of major reports and studies on various aspects of the dire predicament of civilisation; all such reports converge in describing that ecological and human crises have never before been so serious and that the predictions have never been so grave.

In a similar vein to the *Limits to Growth* report is a scientific study from 2015 based on new forms of modelling developed by Anglia Ruskin University's Global Sustainability

Institute, through a project named "Global Resources Observatory." Notably, this report is supported by none other than the British government's Foreign Office among other British insurance companies, banking corporations, an environmental coalition and development banks in Africa and Asia. The report projects that if there is no change in our habits and practices, by the year 2040 industrial civilisation will essentially collapse due to food shortages on an immense scale, propelled by a combination of water scarcity, energy shortages, climate change, and political upheavals.[52]

Since 1947, the Bulletin of Atomic Scientists has annually evaluated nuclear threats, climate change, bio-security and other potential hazards and measured threats to humanity's survival with the Doomsday Clock. In 2015, they set the Doomsday Clock forward two minutes so, for the first time since the Cold War nuclear scare of 1984, the clock now ticks at a mere three minutes to midnight. The Bulletin explains their assessment on the basis that: "international leaders are failing to perform their most important duty—ensuring and preserving the health and vitality of human civilisation."[53]

Also in 2015, in the journal *Science Advances*, a major research study conducted by six international researchers (including none other than Paul R. Ehrlich) reported that we are witnessing a mass extinction of species not seen since the extinction of the dinosaurs 65 million years ago. The loss of biodiversity is one of the most critical current environmental problems, we are told, threatening valuable ecosystem services and human well-being. We are informed that:

"our analysis shows that current extinction rates vastly exceed natural average background rates … We emphasise that our calculations very likely underestimate the severity of the extinction crisis … we can confidently conclude that modern extinction rates are exceptionally high, that they are increasing, and that they suggest a mass extinction under way—the sixth of its kind in Earth's 4.5 billion years of history."[54]

We also witness a massive dislocation of populations, whereby millions have moved from the planet's east to its west and its south to its north, so that, in 2015, some 60 million people were considered refugees, more than at any other time in human history. A major flashpoint of this is the traverse of refugees across the Mediterranean from North Africa to southern Europe in spite of dangerous seas and increasingly militarised borders, of which we were tragically reminded in April with the worst boat disaster of this kind occurring off the island of Lampedusa—800 were confirmed dead. Also in 2015, it was declared that there has been an 80 per cent increase in attempts to make this perilous crossing over the previous year, with such an influx further aggravating urbanisation and the social and economic conditions in various European cities.[55]

There are the long acknowledged causes for such migrations, such as: water shortages, famine from crop failures, economic misery and war; however, as if the Four Horsemen of the Apocalypse needed further accompaniment, these have been joined by the contemporary addition of climate change, a factor with major implications on a global scale which indeed intersects with and exacerbates the classic causes listed above.

A prescient demonstration of this is in research done by the Global Sustainability Institute at Anglia Ruskin University (the same Institute that produced a report discussed earlier) on the systemic causes of the Syrian Revolution and the Civil War; far from issues of the anti-regime political opposition or of Islamic fundamentalism, the study suggested that the underlying causes of the Syrian crisis were water shortages since 2003, partly caused by drought, which had impacted on agricultural productivity, thereby resulting in higher food prices and thus civil unrest.[56]

The several instances of recent scientific research mentioned above are only a partial listing and is over and above the five studies of the UN's International Panel on Climate Change (IPCC) which concluded that our civilisation is the major source of the environmental crisis.

So much for the state's willingness or capacity to move society in an alternative direction. Clearly the political and economic power elites do not see the need and are, in fact, in denial.

The Place and Role of the Environmentalists

Since the power elites are locked up in the logic of state politics and neo-liberal capitalism, what is being done by the many NGOs who labour to affect public policy through the influencing of public opinion? How effective has been the very large wave of concerned citizens who have mobilised for change?

The various publicly known environmental organisations undertake many efforts and campaigns, most of which are isolated, often unofficially competitive with each other, linked only in a sense, and without a deep analysis of our society and consequently without a larger transformative vision. Indeed, the environmental movement is missing a great opportunity in not connecting with other movements that confront different facets of our civilisation's crisis.

Certainly, the environmental movement in past years has demonstrated its resistance most intensely in cities. Mass demonstrations, including civil disobedience, to protest against this or that environmentally destructive government policy or corporate activity have taken place in cities where political and economic power centers are concentrated. Yet it is not only the environmental movement taking to the streets.

In these same cities, in the US for example, sparked in response to police brutality toward blacks, street struggles under the slogan "Black Lives Matter" spontaneously erupted in Ferguson, Oakland and Baltimore, initiated by the urban poor, unemployed, and powerless. Such places, where many of the youth cannot find stable employment, have been devastated by de-industrialisation, class-racial divides and the prison-industrial complex. The post-war gains from fuller employment have, since the 1980s, been appropriated by the plutocracy, while those in the middle of the economic spectrum have been progressively indebted and disenfranchised politically. The underclass, especially those from marginalised ethnic roots and those who are of colour, suffer most from the permanent replacement of labour by virtue of their place at the bottom of society. Such decaying urban landscapes are no "echoes of a dying past" but a picture of our future; recall that economists estimate that around 47%

of presently existing jobs can be automated in the next few decades.

Despite the stark social and economic crisis, there is, nevertheless, a deep divide between the environmentalists and those fighting for social justice. Environmentalists do not seem to seek a convergence with the politically and economically powerless. More generally, there is no visible attempt to bring together the powerless into a social movement with a viable strategy for fundamental change; instead, various protesters work in their respective corners. This divide, needless to say, serves the interest of the 1%, leaving so much potential political momentum fragmented and demobilised.

The one exception to this pattern has been the attempt to create a web of networks working within the framework of the social forums, the zenith of which is the biennial World Social Forums traditionally held in the global South and replicated in numerous forms at national, regional and local levels across the world. And while in this milieu there is an anti-capitalist ethos, the strategy for a political or economic alternative is not clearly visible.[57]

Beyond Protest and Toward Community Building

To be a force for fundamental social change we must evolve intellectually and politically, especially in Europe and North America; we must move beyond treading the water of activist routines like street protests, vigils, activist training camps, publishing books or zines, web and social media strategies, and attendance at book fairs or seminars. Sometimes, environmentalists are even involved in heroic symbolism, but the question remains: what strategy is there beyond protests? We know that the police and their agents can be outsmarted by young people in various street manoeuvres or surprise banner drops on iconic sites. We also know that direct action, especially if it is on a large scale, is a reliable means to force concessions from both the state and corporations.

True, such tactics have made us aware of our strength, but we have yet to develop the means to use them to their full potential. On their own they cannot deliver fundamental change; they must be part of a contextualised social movement that stresses coherence, common direction and goals. We can and do force the state to make token reforms, but the old patterns of power politics return the moment that the protesters go home and the mass media start their regular news coverage. To go beyond protest, we need an alternative programmatic prospective or politics and a subsequent organising strategy. In the project to create a genuine new politics, we have to face the question of how we can bring people, specifically as citizens, together to form or regenerate community.

It is the contention of this book that the ecological crisis demands urgent systemic change, which is to say challenging and transcending a profit-centric economic system based on ruthless competition and growth for its own sake. We must replace capitalism and the nation-state with a new society that values humanity and nature over materialism and its products. Radical change like this requires radical anger—but is it enough that such anger is merely ritually vented in momentary displays of protest?

The New Politics of Social Ecology

The major problem facing today's activists is that they are not radical enough. They do not know how to turn anger and frustration in the streets into a more permanent expression of popular power. The institutionalisation of popular rage should not be our goal; on the contrary, we must amplify the impact of this anger by creating a durable and well organised radical base through community organisation. A sustained challenge to political and economic authority in order to effect fundamental systemic change can only occur by building such an alternative power structure with geographic expressions.

What is needed is building the blocks of community organising with everyday citizens, and especially the powerless, to overcome capitalist urbanisation's fragmentation of our society, to discover our force in numbers and so imagine alternative worlds that such solidarity can build—this is applied politics. We need to also connect to the larger public realm of the neighbourhood and the city, recognising these as strategic political terrains. Suffice to say for now that the development of community in the megalopolitan context must be preceded by urban neighbourhoods and, within each of these, a network of local, democratic counter-institutions which have to be developed through community organisations. The premise of such a strategy is that we should consciously choose to be deeply based in our neighbourhoods while also embracing surrounding community and social concerns.

We should be identified for who we are and for what we stand for. We begin by listening, by being sensitive to all the important concerns of the surrounding people in the area, to their feelings and preoccupations. In neighbourhoods, a place to start is to make every effort to know one's neighbors and thus to promote new social relations, new forms of civic action and more self-determination, all of which can take many different forms; our neighbourhoods, seemingly quotidian, are full of untapped potential for social change. With time we must identify with the most imaginative and visionary of the people's social concerns.

This is important to think about now because it is obvious that the current upswing in the cycle of struggle will not subside any time soon. The underlying causes of widespread unrest—large scale environmental degradation, institutional racism, economic injustice and growing inequality—are the pillars of contemporary capitalism which will have only a more intense effect as the system slips into greater crisis. An increasingly large portion of the population will necessarily be radicalised by these pressures. Whether they turn to the radical Left or the nationalist and fascist Right will depend on the ability of radical social bases to offer a viable strategy which can deliver meaningful changes to the structure, culture and basic values of society.

EPILOGUE

1993

The ecology movement is part of history in the making. Environmental degradation is a highly tangible problem; millions of people can see, smell, taste and hear it. Given the immediacy and magnitude of the problem, it is not surprising that the ecology movement is diverse. It is also unregimented—people move in, around and out of it. But it will continue to exist and grow in one form or another. It constitutes an ever present potential, especially insofar as it marks a shift from an overweening emphasis on material values and individual security toward a regard for the quality of life. This is especially significant in the northern hemisphere, the primary polluting engine of the world. The traditional models of economic growth, whether capitalist or state socialist, are being fundamentally challenged by political ecologists, as are the dominant values of productivism and consumerism.

But there are creatures that linger fatally in warm water slowly coming to a boil. The human species is an example of this. Will we make the right choice in time? So far, the action taken has been palliative at best. The political and economic structures of modern states are overgrown and do not respond adequately to organised public pressure. Moreover, the people with the power to effect the sweeping changes necessary to preserving our planet are often beholden to special interests driven above all by the profit motive, regardless of its long term consequences. Thus, as we have argued, the state management of the ecological crisis has not substantially retarded the pace of environmental destruction, let alone reversed the course toward ecocide. The Earth Summit in Rio (1993) was an illustration of this dead-end.

Therefore, we have a choice. On the hand, there is the creation of a global super-state based on a world capitalist economy that attempts to regulate the environment and minimise the worst impacts of the international war system; *or* there is the program of political ecology and, more specifically, the radical philosophy and politics of social ecology which demands the patient renovation and reconstruction of human society from the ground up to build a free world.

Listen to the grass growing—think globally, act locally.
Da capo!

EPILOGUE

2015

At a time when a blind driving machine called the market is turning soil into sand, covering fertile land with concrete, poisoning air and water, and producing sweeping climatic and atmospheric changes, we are forced to pose fundamental questions about the nature of our society. This book is an attempt to grapple with the ecological crisis, on the one hand, and the aggrieved state of modern society, on the other. We cannot ignore the structures of oppression or repression in our society, the concentration of power in hierarchy and class and the systemic addiction to greed, all of which are dominant factors beneath the headlines of the social and ecological crises.

The events of the month of July, 2015 are a particular case in point. The brutal power of capital and the political elite that control the Eurozone were at their vicious worst when they descended on Greece during the weekend of 10-12 July, 2015. Rarely has the naked force of neoliberalism been so visibly displayed. Draconian economic and political conditions were almost unilaterally imposed on a country, a demonstration that the era of national sovereignty is a line of defense in the past. This show-case of the neoliberal "shock doctrine" was also a clear warning to other European political parties and countries that international finance capitalism will not permit them to step out of line.

In the face of Eurozone blackmail, Greece has been inflicted by austerity policies as if it were a neoliberal laboratory of the Eurocrats. Indeed, despite the arrival of a radical left-wing Greek government, the hope of the European anti-austerity movement, this very same government quietly surrendered after less than six months in power; the agreement accepted by the Syriza government was exactly what a national referendum had rejected by a majority of some 61% of the voting public less than a week before. The dictates of international finance thus ensured that the arrogant power of foreign bureaucrats and politicians determined the political direction of the country totally in spite of an explicit democratic expression of popular sentiment. And yet, there was no consistent mass opposition by the people in the streets and public places against the government's reversal of the referendum results.

This case shows, if nothing else, that the power of genuine national sovereignty barely exists within the totalising capitalist world order: in environmental policy as much as in financial policy. The only effective defense against the brutal power of such capitalism is if civil society is radically organised so that citizens occupy public places and buildings where the 1% exercise their power and so attempt to reorganise the whole power structure of society. The power of citizens can now only be demonstrated through mass action by the people from the neighbourhoods and cities aimed at confronting the state, forming a line of defense against outside manipulation, destabilising neoliberal corporate dominance and reclaiming the people's self-determination.

Whether such action amounts to a social revolution is a matter for others to analyze and determine. What comes to mind is what once was named "the commune of communes" in the tradition of the Paris Commune. In taking such a direction, the overarching politics could be best provided by the politics of social ecology and its fundamental commitment to direct democracy. This could mean, in turn, that mediated politics would have to come to an end; citizens through their own local assemblies would speak and decide for themselves rather than through professional politicians. Once this process is engaged, its success and duration would depend upon the practice of a new "democratic confederalism" whereby cities and regions work together to advance the common good, socio-politically and economically. To be sure, such a process will by necessity and ethics be based on much struggle and organisation which may even involve civil disobedience and non-violet direct action in defiance of a relentless system.

There is no avoiding imagining new and different scenarios than the status quo. Surely another world is possible.

POSTSCRIPT

After Paris COP21 – What Next? System Change not Climate Change

February 2016

Paris, in the first two weeks of December 2015, hosted the 21st Conference of the Parties (COP21) of the United Nations Framework Convention on Climate Change (UNFCCC). The global environmental conference of the decade saw many heads of state and national ministers of the environment, and an entraining army of their bureaucrats and professional negotiators, NGOs and UN staff, converge in a massive complex at Le Bourget in the outer suburbs of Paris. On December 13th, after two weeks and many late nights of wrangling over the draft text, the 32 page final document was read to a standing ovation at the closing ceremony. An historic agreement it was not, although, for the first time since scientists first warned us of climate change in the 1960s, the State bureaucrats of the world unanimously and officially admitted that the science was real and urgent action necessary. The denial was over.

Paris was still very much a police state, with armed military swarming the city, as the state of emergency following the November terrorist attacks was still active. Nevertheless, two massive demonstrations took place at which the popular slogan, "System change, not climate change!" was powerfully proclaimed and the final Paris Agreement was criticised as grossly inadequate.

What does the new 35 page agreement mean for the future of the planet? One could see the fingerprints of the fossil fuel companies all over the final text. Scientists who closely monitored the talks in Paris said it was not the agreement that humanity really needed. In an interview with *The Guardian*, James Hansen, himself the father of climate science and former head of the NASA Goddard Institute for Space Studies, described it as a "fraud". He added:

> It's just bullshit for them to say: 'We'll have a 2C warming target and then try to do a little better every five years.' It's just worthless words. There is no action, just promises. As long as fossil fuels appear to be the cheapest fuels out there, they will be continued to be burned.

Surprise, surprise: this agreement, by itself, will not turn the dramatic global climate situation around.

In addition to accepting the reality of climate change and the urgent need for action, states agreed to try to limit warming to 2 degrees Celsius (°C) by 2100 from pre-industrial levels, with mention of "efforts" to aim for 1.5 °C. (Saudi Arabia was obstructionist to the latter, more ambitious, target and still refuses to acknowledge it.) It was also agreed to aim to peak emissions as soon as possible and to achieve net-zero emissions in the very vague timeframe of "the second half of the 21st Century"; moreover, the use of jargon like 'net-zero emissions' suggests an avoidance of directly cutting emissions and a subtle shift to attempting to compensate for it through fanciful technology and scam-prone emissions offsets schemes.

Celebrating the agreement as 'legally binding' is a vast exaggeration as the only mandatory aspect is that states must measure and report on their emissions every five years, starting in 2018, though they will be encouraged to increase ("ratchet up") their targets. The commitments of states to emissions reductions are entirely voluntary, appropriately given the wishy washy and obscure name 'Intended Nationally Determined Contributions' (INDCs) (these become 'Nationally Determined Contributions' (NDCs) once the country signs onto the Paris Agreement), and there are no penalties for not adhering to such targets.

Despite the vigorous rhetoric of states' stirring speeches at the opening session of COP21, it is officially estimated that the sum of all of the states' INDCs will lead to warming of between 2.3 °C and 3.5 °C by 2100, a catastrophic situation which the final text itself admits is far beyond 2 °C let alone 1.5 °C. This is assuming that these targets are met, for which there is little hope given the pathetic history of state commitments to climate action; in fact, current policies would see an estimated warming of between 2.6 °C and an astronomical 4.9 °C.[58] A warming of even half of the latter is predicted by some to result in the collapse of civilisation. A warming of only 2 °C means a 50/50 chance of runaway climate change, a situation that is disturbing enough.

Even liberal environmentalists like Bill McKibben felt unsatisfied in the end with the agreement and states' "modest" voluntary commitments. In a column in the New York Times, immediately following the close of COP21, he complained:

> So the world emerges, finally, with something like a climate accord, albeit unenforceable. If all parties kept their promises, the planet would warm up by an estimated 6.3 °F, or 3.5 °C, above preindustrial levels. And that is way, way too much. We are set to pass the 1 °C mark this year, and that's already enough to melt ice caps and push the sea level threateningly higher.[59]

Another outcome was the commitment to setup an Adaptation Fund of $100 billion by 2020 to help poorer and more vulnerable countries adapt to the effects of climate change. However, contributions to this fund are entirely voluntary (only a fraction has so far been committed, $10 billion as of April 2017) and it is feared that states will take this funding from existing aid budgets.

The concept of 'compensation for loss and damage'—recognising the liability of richer, polluting countries for climate change impacts upon poorer, less polluting countries—was ruled out as it was contested by powerful states like the US and the EU. Thus, poorer states affected by climate change will not be able to seek compensation from the richer countries who have a greater historical responsibility in what Lumumba Di-Aping, Sudan's chief climate negotiator to COP15 in Copenhagen, has described as the "'colonisation of the sky".

Furthermore, international aviation and shipping are entirely excluded from the agreement; as they occur internationally, they aren't even counted under any state's emissions nor are they dealt with by the UNFCCC. This is despite the fact that they currently account for 8% of global emissions and are set to increase 270% by 2050, at which time they could account for 40% of global emissions.[60]

Due to opposition from the US, the EU and Norway, language for human rights appears only in the preamble, preventing it from being legally binding, a fact that ironically emerged on Human Rights Day. Equally shocking, these same states ensured that all mention of indigenous rights was also totally removed from the Decision text and relegated to the merely symbolic preamble, despite the fact that indigenous peoples are estimated to protect 80% of biodiversity. The prospect of real indigenous rights could pose a potential threat to privatisation and mega-projects by blocking mining, land grabbing and apparently 'green' projects like hydro-electric dams and the privatisation of forests for carbon credits under REDD+ (Reducing Emissions from Deforestation and Forest Degradation). According to Dallas Goldtooth, an organizer for the US-based Indigenous Environmental Network:

> To be absolutely frank, [for] our organization and [for] me personally, I'm not surprised that our rights as Indigenous Peoples are one of the most contentious and the ones that get left out of the agreement. It just goes to show that our political leaders are not truly concerned about the value of human diversity, human life or mother earth — they're concerned about maintaining business as usual.[61]

On the 11th hour before the international agreement was concluded and adopted on Saturday December 12th, a single word threatened to derail years of discussions of calculated negotiations and two weeks of high powered diplomacy. That developed countries "shall" undertake economy-wide absolute emission reduction targets was perceived as too strong by the US, who began to cause a fuss at the last moment to ensure it be changed into the more watery "should", which is a world away in international law. Eventually, to avoid re-opening up the text to other revisions and more lengthy debate, the French presidency quietly slipped through the change of "shall" to "should" without debate by passing it off as the typographic error of an anonymous sleep deprived negotiating team.[62]

The United Nations process moves ahead. The Paris Agreement's financing provisions will only kick in during 2020. The 55 countries with the most emissions, representing at least 55 percent of total greenhouse emissions, were invited to sign on in an Earth Day ceremony at the United Nations headquarters in New York on April 22, 2016, thus officially activating the agreement. Ultimately, 174 countries and the European Union signed on, with US Secretary of State,

John Kerry, prompting a swelling of sighs as he carried his granddaughter by the hip onto the stage, one of 197 children (representing all the states of the world) in attendance at the event. It was bizarrely tender for a ceremony of no consequence for the future of the planet.[63]

On the one hand, the Paris deal seems to set a high target, declaring that the global average temperature rise ought to be kept 'well below' 2 °C, and that countries shall pursue efforts to limit warming to 1.5 °C. Scientists say that the first target would require that industrial emissions of greenhouse gases come to an end by roughly 2050 and, for the second target, by about 2030. However, the infrastructure for fossil fuel power plants, refineries, mines and pipelines are being built today that can be expected to operate well past 2050; meanwhile, fossil-fuel companies are spending hundreds of billions of dollars a year looking for new reserves that must not be burned if either target is to be met. Furthermore, free trade agreements are ploughing ahead, giving corporations unprecedented power to bully states that try to limit polluting international trade. A serious campaign to meet the more ambitious goal would mean that, in less than two decades, the nation-states of the world would probably have to bring an end to gasoline fueled cars, to coal or gas-burning power plants in their current form, and to airplanes or ships powered by fossil fuels. Countries have offered no plans that would come remotely close to achieving either goal and, given the current level of technology, it is difficult to see how such goals could be achieved.

The great ice sheets remain imperiled, the oceans are still rising filled with fields of floating garbage, the poorest countries are being lashed by heat waves and floods, bushfires and hurricanes, and the agriculture system that feeds seven billion people is at risk as the multinational corporations that dominate food production continue to drive a singular monoculture submerged in chemical fertilisers.

The two-week UN climate change conference in Paris focused on many physical dangers associated with climate change: extreme weather, severe drought, the warming of the oceans, rain forest destruction and disruptions of the food supply. But global warming has also had another effect – the large scale displacement of people – a theme that was an ominous, politically sensitive shadow over the Paris talks and side events. 2015 was a year of unprecedented flows of refugees, especially from Syria to Lebanon, Jordan and Turkey, and from the latter to Greece and Eastern Europe towards Western and Northern Europe. A drought that lasted from 2006 to 2011 in much of Syria has been cited as a factor in the long-running civil war responsible for this mass migration.[64]

While there was rhetoric, evoking a sense of urgency, in the official Blue Zone negotiating area, the international agreement's obligations for signatory states do not even come into effect until 2020. Fifty years ago the first warning on global warming was put on the desks of heads of state and quickly forgotten. The current politico-economic world system is simply too slow in facing reality. Some progress may take place with COP21 behind us but it is all too little, too late. Another direction is urgently needed.

Greenhouse gas emissions – primarily of carbon dioxide from the burning of fossil fuels and the destruction of forests – have been rising for decades, interrupted only briefly by economic downturns. They stalled in 2015, projected to fall 0.8 percent in part because of the softness of the Chinese economy. Yet December, the very month of COP21, was the warmest December on record, bringing bizarrely pleasant weather to international delegates in Paris during the conference and a Christmas Eve in Montréal, my city, of plus 15 °C when it should have been between minus three and minus ten. Indeed, according to the UK's Met Office, NASA and the National Oceanic and Atmospheric Administration (NOAA), 2015 was the hottest year in recorded history, breaking a benchmark set only one year earlier. All ten of the hottest years in a global record stretching from 1880 have occurred since 1998. No one under 30 has ever lived through a single month of global temperatures below the 20th Century average.[65] In fact, since the year 2000, the vast majority of months have had an average temperature of at least 0.5 °C warmer than the 20th Century average. Such dramatic climatic changes are not merely special cases; our industrial civilisation is such that it is ushering in a fundamentally new moment in the history of the planet.

A New Geological Era

In 2014, the fifth report of the IPCC (the International Panel on Climate Change, involving some 3000 scientists worldwide) categorically declared what politicians and bureaucrats have, for too long, been ignoring: namely that it is extremely likely that human influence has been the dominant cause of global warming since 1950 ("extremely likely", in IPCC parlance, denotes 95-100% probability, an upgrade from "very likely"—a 90-100% probability—which was used in the 2007 IPCC Fourth Assessment Report). Could this be even shaping the geological destiny of the planet?

The history of the Earth is divided into geological epochs of thousands of millions of years, each marked by a biological, climatic or seismic event, as reflected in the Earth and its sedimentary layers. We are currently living in what is usually classified as the Holocene which began 11,500 years ago and permitted the emergence of agriculture and settlement living. However, our environmental footprint is so great that there is growing consensus that such a geological categorisation is now obsolete given the extraordinary impact that human civilisation is having on the Earth: an increase in the global temperature, the most rapid mass extinction of species since the dinosaurs and ocean acidification, to name just a few. Such unprecedented phenomena seems to be shifting even the Earth's geological structure.

We are surrounded by industrial areas, highways, cities, suburban housing developments, as well as pasture lands and planted forests. While such artificial areas composed only 5% of the Earth's surface in 1750, they now represent almost one third. Other less noticeable natural disruptions are also at work. Ninety percent of photosynthesis on Earth today is carried out by ecosystems which have been altered by humans. For the last 150 years, new chemicals and substances such as plastic or endocrine disruptors have been added to the biosphere, leaving their mark upon even sediments and developing fossils. Far from being inevitable, these effects have been determined by the political, economic, and ideological choices made by a small proportion of humanity.

"Human activities have become so pervasive and profound that they rival the great forces of nature and are pushing the Earth into planetary terra incognita," explains Paul Crutzen, fifteen years ago to an audience of scientists. The Nobel Prize Laureate in chemistry exclaims, at the height of his voice: "We are no longer in the Holocene but the Anthropocene!" 'Anthropocene' is a newly coined term derived from the Greek 'anthropos' (human) and 'kainos' (recent or new); it illustrates how the human race has become a geological force influencing land, sea, fauna, flora and the climate in the same way that primordial tectonic, asteroidal, volcanic and atmospheric forces have shaped the Earth. Such is the effect of humanity on the planet that, for Crutzen, it warrants an entirely new categorisation in the Geological Time Scale. However, is it not insufficient to merely analyse the extraordinary effect of human civilisation in shaping the natural environment without also drawing a link to the extreme economic system that it is yoked to, indeed driven by? How can we philosophise vaguely about the Anthropocene without diagnosing capitalism and its forces of greed and competition, hierarchy and exploitation, as the real roots of the crisis?

Over the last two centuries, a model of industrial development based on fossil fuels has not only changed our planet's geological path, but it has also developed profound inequalities. According to Christophe Bonneuil, in the article "Tous responsables ?" ("Are We All Responsible?") in *Le Monde Diplomatique*:

Despite many destructive wars, capital grew by a factor of 134 between 1700 and 2008. Is it not this drive for accumulation that propelled the Earth's transformation? So wouldn't the Anthropocene actually be more fittingly described as the 'Capitalocene'? ... The poorest 20% (200 million people) received 4.7% of global income in 1820 but only 2.2% in 1992 (though this income bracket had by then grown to over a billion people). Is there a link between the history of inequalities and the history of the global ecological degradation of the anthropocene? "No," respond the advocates of 'green capitalism', who blithely insist on the old 'win-win' discourse of 'market', 'growth', 'social equity' and 'environment'. Yet many recent studies on the history and sciences of the Earth system are challenging this, revealing a common engine driving global economic and social domination, environmental injustice and ecological disruption.[66]

So is it not a deception to analyse the Anthropocene separate from the 'C Word'—'Capitalism'—thus naturalising the ecological catastrophe as a natural part of planetary evolution?

All human activity changes the environment but its impact is distributed vastly unevenly. The nations that have produced the most are the economically 'central' countries that have historically dominated the world economy. Based largely in these economically central countries are 90 companies that are responsible for more than 63% of global greenhouse gas emissions since 1850. This certainly includes the UK which, during the Victorian era of the 19th Century, produced half of the total global carbon emissions and colonised the world.[67] These corporations are the pioneers, the standard-bearers, of this age of the Capitalocene. Indeed, they are well aware of the threat that questions of climate action poses to their business model, not to mention the basic logic and structure of capitalist civilisation. So nervous are they of the dramatic implications of this that they scrambled to be major stakeholders in COP21, mobilising sizeable financial resources and a fully fledged marketing assault precisely as a way to set the agenda—a COP21 forged in the Babylonian image of corporate capitalism.

A Pact With the Devil

United Nations climate conferences have been marked, since their very beginning, by the State's alliance with the agents of market capitalism as their partner in 'managing' the climate crisis.[68] COP21 indicates an even more invigorated emphasis on this alliance, a pact with the Devil rudely demonstrated by the cabal of polluting multinationals directly involved in the official conference.

The conference was sponsored left, right and centre by big, and mostly French, corporations who are intimately involved in the pollution of the planet. Suez Environment is a serial agent of water privatisation, especially in the Global South, as well as part of a pro-fracking lobby. Engie and Generali are huge financers of coal and dirty energy. EDF pushes coal in the Global South and BNP Paribas is the largest coal financer in France. In the car industry, Renault Nissan and Bollore are pro-nuclear and Michelin is involved in land grabs in the Global South. In the airline industry, Air France pushes forest

After Paris COP21 – What Next?

offsets and fights tougher measures on aviations emissions while Aéroports de Paris uses highly polluting technologies in its airports. La Caisse des Dépots heavily invests in polluting sectors while AXA speculates on climate-related disasters.[69]

Does this sponsorship seem strange, even schizophrenic, given that the business models of these very corporations are deeply responsible for climate change? On the one hand, at the national level, fossil fuel corporations are usually actively hostile to climate policymaking, even funding elaborate media campaigns of outright climate denialism. On the other hand, at the international level, they present themselves as actively engaged in developing solutions, enthusiastically 'partnering with' (read: bankrolling) climate conferences to influence the official narrative about climate action, to gain PR credit through greenwashing and to distract from their climate crimes. With the failure of government policy-making and the resulting inertia of climate change negotiations, intergovernmental climate agencies like the UNFCCC have readily welcomed these multinationals by rolling out the red carpet, praising them as a central part of the solution and

celebrating the promise of 'green growth'. Such multinationals lap up the attention, promoting techno-fix and market solutions to subtly sidetrack or delay real action that would directly challenge polluters.

The intimacy of corporations with the UN climate negotiations process has a history. On the eve of the 1992 Rio Earth Summit, the very beginning of the UNFCCC, the World Business Council on Sustainable Development (WBCSD) was formed by multinationals such as Shell, Volkswagen, BP, Monsanto, Total and Dow Chemicals "to ensure the business voice was heard." Eight years later, the WBCSD and its corporate members teamed up with the UN Conference on Trade and Development and other corporations such as Shell, Rio Tinto and KPMG to form the International Emissions Trading Association (IETA) to promote the magic of the market and the great fraud of emissions trading as a solution to the climate crisis. Together, the WBCSD and IETA, along with the International Chamber of Commerce, three corporate archangels of false solutions, have been increasingly present at UN climate and environmental summits, even being actively courted to co-organise and sponsor them.[70]

This has become particularly flagrant in recent years such as at the 2009 COP15 in Copenhagen when IETA had 500 of its corporate members accredited to official negotiations; this was the same conference where hundreds of NGOs were abruptly evicted *en masse* from the conference centre, including all ninety delegates of Friends of the Earth, because of a peaceful protest inside the conference that raised issues of climate justice and the interests of the poor.[71] Then there was the infamous COP19 in Warsaw in 2013, where fossil fuel businesses were official sponsors of the talks and the Polish Government even organised, with the World Coal Association, a coal and climate summit on the sidelines, despite massive civil society opposition.

In 2014, UN Secretary-General Ban Ki-moon organised his own climate summit at the UN in New York City that, among other things, celebrated the role of business, with a special emphasis on the banking and financial industry. Soon after, the Lima-Paris Action Agenda launched at Lima COP20 outlined how to formally include big business in the UN climate framework. It was integrated into the Paris Accord where big business climate commitments were even lauded alongside the official negotiated outcome.[72]

The former Executive Secretary (between 2010-2016) of the UNFCCC Secretariat herself, Christiana Figueres, demonstrates the intimacy between the corporations and UN climate policymaking. Before taking up her UNFCCC post, she worked as the 'Principal Climate Change Advisor' to Latin America's largset private energy utility, ENDESA Latinoamérica. As well as speaking at the infamous coal and climate summit in Warsaw, she is a regular at IETA's annual Carbon Expo. In May 2015, she even publicly attacked those who claim that the fossil fuel industry is not part of the solution, imploring such critics to: "Stop demonising oil and gas companies." The revolving door between the top position in the UNFCCC and multinational corporates is not exclusive to Figueres. Her predecessor, Yvo de Boer, after presiding over the dramatic failure of COP15 Copenhagen in 2009, soon quit to work as a consultant for the accounting multinational KPMG as the Special Global Advisor on Climate Change and

Sustainability. Later, the infamous World Economic Forum, the infamous convergence of the global rich and powerful, appointed him to chair its Global Agenda Council on Climate Change.[73]

At COP21, there was a frenzy of corporate climate conferences and exhibition fairs, the three most notable being 'Open For Business Hub' inside the official negotiations, the exclusive business space 'La Galerie des solutions' organised by the official COP21 with big business, and 'Solutions COP21', a corporate expo at the Grand Palais. The French Government, in a bid to outsource 20 per cent of the total conference funding, roped in some of the most polluting private companies on the planet, many of whom are French.[74] Thus, the logos of champion polluters adorned the walls of the Conference during the two weeks of the Summit. Instead of averting climate catastrophe, the COPs have increasingly been serving as exhibitions and promotional fairs for the world's shadiest environmental criminals. At such events, where the cost of having a kiosk goes into the hundreds of thousands of dollars, there are several false solutions which are, by now, recurring themes.

Either it is lauding nuclear power or natural gas—both conventional and fracked—as clean alternatives to coal and oil. Or it is insisting on the power of the 'invisible hand of the market' through magical mechanisms like carbon taxes or emissions trading schemes, where corporations, through what could be called 'creative accounting', offset their emissions through obscure programs of carbon credits. In a moment when it is clear that 80 percent of fossil fuel reserves must stay in the ground, these often tried and failed measures only weaken the emphasis on ending the exploitation of fossil fuels and massively investing in renewable energy and public transport.[75]

Then there are the silver bullets of risky and yet to be discovered techno-fixes to suck CO2 from the atmosphere (while leaving emitting industries unchallenged) justified by the idea of aiming for 'net-zero emissions'. Such measures include fantasy technologies like 'carbon capture and storage' (capturing carbon emissions and injecting it deep underground), or strategies that would result in extensive land grabbing for tree plantations or for growing agrofuels (which uses food staples, such as corn, for expensive biofuels, thus driving up the cost of food for the poor). Then there is the notoriously risky terrain of geo-engineering with hubristic sci-fi fantasies like pumping sulfur into the atmosphere, erecting giant mirrors in outer space or growing carbon-devouring algae in the seas.

Let's not forgot the agricultural industry, where the usual suspects in the fields of food retail, seeds and fertilisers (including Monsanto, Syngenta and Yara) laud the advent of biotechnology and 'climate smart agriculture'. This nifty sounding concept means what you want it to: genetically modified seeds, intensive monocultural farming and synthetic fertiliser production, the latter of which is a hugely intensive emitter, especially of nitrous oxide, and is the consumer of the majority of US fracked natural gas.

The corporations unashamed capture of COP21 was satirised by Brandalism (their name is a joining of 'brand' and 'vandalism'). This was a clever art project that involved UK-based artists replacing advertising stands around Le

Bourget with fake advertising posters that satirically mocked the hypocrisy of key corporations and world leaders involved in the official COP21 conference.[76]

Added to this corporate influence and power is the whole 'free trade' framework which, through a series of international treaties, multi-national corporations now have the legal power to contest before the courts any law or public policy adopted by legislatures within national territories of which, according to these companies, interfere with 'free trade'. At the same time as the climate change legal framework is frustratingly weak and powerless, free trade treaties are enforcing laws that are an unprecedented attack on the sovereignty of the State whilst empowering multinational corporations in international trade tribunals; whilst the Paris Agreement is only 35 pages, free trade treaties usually go into the thousands of pages.

National, regional and municipal governments have been disarmed in many areas of public policy such as environmental protection measures that they may adopt; corporations can even sue states for measures that threaten, or have even blocked, their polluting projects on the basis of "revenue lost". For example, after years of indigenous groups, environmentalists and farmers fighting against it, TransCanada threatened using the terms of the North American Free Trade Agreement (NAFTA) treaty to sue the Obama Administration for $15 billion for its veto of the Keystone XL pipeline. And yet the poor of the world will not be able to seek compensation when they are severely affected by climate change.[77]

At COP21, it was openly admitted that states are unable

to effect the change needed and that the major multinational corporations must drive the collective effort. When the State seeks direction and solutions from the infamous multinationals who are profiting from and driving the polluting world economy, we know that the state management of the environment has failed.

COP21 in Paris saw participation on five different levels: the exclusive Blue Zone for negotiations, the Green Zone, the Climate Summit for Local Leaders, the Festival of Alternatives in Montreuil and the Climate Action Zone and its associated demonstrations. In the Blue Zone at Le Bourget, a massive convention hall and the main focus of international media attention, were one hundred heads of state as well as 40 000 delegates composed of state negotiators, the army of bureaucrats that assisted them and the lobbyists of both multinational corporations and NGOs. There was also the publicly accessible Green Zone, designed with the consultation of civil society, which featured major NGOs, foundations and some city and regional governments, as well as companies promoting their technological solutions and elements of civil society to organise workshops and discussions.

Municipalism and the Right to the City

In addition to these two streams of activity, the third stream was the gathering of municipalities, a highly significant act that valorises the power of action at the local level across a global scale. Hosted by the Mayor of Paris, Anne Hidalgo, a thousand mayors from across the world descended on Hotel de Ville for 'Climate Summit for Local Leaders: Cities for Climate' to discuss the role of cities in climate change. In statements made by mayors in the bustling opening session, amidst the architectural grandeur of City Hall, there was a general consensus that cities are best suited to deal with climate change given that both 70% of emissions come from cities and moreover that cities have more of a proximity to the people.

One of the more interesting moments of this conference was a round table discussion titled: 'From COP21 to Habitat III: Local Governments and Citizens at the Heart of the Challenge' organised by the 'Commission on Social Inclusion, Participatory Democracy and Human Rights' of United Cities and Local Governments (UCLG), the largest worldwide federation of cities.[78] It was appropriately hosted north of Paris in St. Denis where the suburbs like it are boiling with issues of inequality, and racial divisions. These are traditionally left-wing municipalities. This round table aimed at bringing questions of social justice and equality into the question of ecology and, in particular, valorising the role of cities. Notable were the contributions of radical municipalities, such as Barcelona, Bogota, Madrid, Saint-Denis and Le Courneuve (north of Paris), Grenoble and Gwangju as well as a collection of civil society organisations like Alternatiba, Coalition Climat 21, Collectif des associations des citoyens, AITEC and Observatorio DESC (an observatory of economic, social and cultural rights).

Such radical municipalities and organisations questioned the logic of neoliberalism, the logic of the city as a business, and insisted that issues of inequality, discrimination, ecological crisis and social breakdown are all interconnected. They insisted not only on the need to confront neoliberalism, to democratise cities and to deal with inequality, but they articulated noteworthy system changes. This perspective was refreshing with much radical potential, yet such discourses were unimaginable in the Blue or Green Zones. There, also, circulated the concept of the 'Right to the City', a claim of the collective right of citizens to democratically determine the destiny of their cities against the power of business and authoritarian governance. This is has been officially adopted by the UCLG, though it remains to be seen whether it is unanimously promoted or even understood by all cities and bureaucratic levels in the UCLG.

At a moment when the discussion seemed to be stranded as to what to do regarding the domination of city streets by the automobile, I raised the concept of the need for cities to introduce free public transport, rendering it a right rather than a paid service. Lorena Zarate, President of the Habitat International Coalition (HIC), powerfully critiqued the neoliberal model of cities and its dispossession of the poor. She also highlighted the 'Global Platform for the Right to the City', an international Right to the City network that lobbies the UN and the UCLG.[79]

Barcelona's Mayor Ada Colau, a radical grassroots activist who emerged from the citizen housing rights organisation Plataforma de Afectados por la Hipoteca (PAH—translated as 'Platform for People Affected by Mortgages') was actively present. PAH is the most successful housing rights movement in Europe. It is organised through horizontal assemblies of residents who are affected by evictions based on collective solidarity; it practices direct action through squatting homes to be repossessed and occupying the banks involved in the attempted repossession.

Montreuil: The Village of Alternatives

The fourth stream of COP21 occurred in the city of Montreuil, a politically and culturally important municipality to the east of Paris. There the 'Village des alternatives' saw a huge gathering of European civil society organisations and movements offering alternatives to both capitalism and the State. For four months in the lead up to COP21, the Alternatiba Movement had organised a nationwide cycle tour travelling from city to city around France, raising the question of climate change and the need for fundamental transformation of our society through grassroots democracy and ecological transition. With the support of the left-wing municipality of the city of Montreuil, the Alternatiba Movement was able to organise a large festival to mark the end of their journey. This festival was composed of a street fair with hundreds of stalls of activist organisations from across France and Europe under categories such as housing, energy, transport, food, culture, media, and migration. These ranged from those who challenged market capitalism's focus on growth for the sake of growth whilst others stressed cooperative and ecological alternatives—an anti-profit economy based on human needs and solidarity. Many sought to reverse the dominant ideology of productionism. Le Monde Libertaire newspaper of the French Anarchist Federation had a prominent presence. There was even a main stage for concerts and a kitchen for cheap but healthy vegan food cooked onsite.

At the same time there was an enormous program of hundreds of self-organised workshops, in the same style as the World Social Forum, that touched on diverse topics. I spoke at an important panel in the town hall of Montreuil City Hall organised by UCLG which dealt with the question of: 'The Ecological Transition and the Right to the City', bringing together eight speakers who were left-wing municipal politicians, researchers, social movement organisers. They made the connection between the 'Right to the City' and the ecological transition. It was well received with over a 150 people in attendance. Important questions were raised about whether an ecological transition is possible without democratising our societies at the local, and especially urban, level. Another highlight of the Montreuil festival was an electrifying panel where Naomi Klein and Jeremy Corbyn joined forces with unions to talk about energy democracy—an important sign of much needed collaboration between the climate movement and the traditional workers' movement.

The Climate Action Zone

When the weekend at Montreuil finished, many of the social movement activists migrated to the Zone d'action climat (Climate Action Zone), organised by Climate Coalition 21, which I see as the fifth stream of COP21, along with the many demonstrations and direct actions that radiated out of this. It was held at the Centre Centquartre, an old warehouse converted into a conference space. Similar to Montreuil, this World Social Forum format was characterised by many self-organised workshops. A public meeting of over 3000 attended a panel discussion, with Naomi Klein, about the threat of free trade agreements for the climate as the featured speaker. She made a rousing statement denouncing capitalism and its neo-liberal manifestation in free trade agreements and offered a course of action based on protest and direct action, including occupations. Certainly, with the activist movements essentially excluded from the official proceedings of COP21 and left out in the cold while state bureaucrats, surrounded by corporate lobbyists, determine the future of the planet, the only recourse is vocal and effective protest actions. And among the most exemplary of these actions were led by indigenous people.

Indigenous Peoples Rising

Although mention of indigenous people was eventually cut from the Decision Text, indigenous peoples were well represented in Paris, on the frontlines at marches and at Le Bourget. In the Green Zone, the civilian area of the Le Bourget COP21 complex, the International Indigenous Peoples Forum on Climate Change (IIPFCC) organised an indigenous pavilion with well-coordinated events and talks throughout COP21. Here, at a press conference, indigenous leaders from Africa, Asia, and Latin America revealed that over 20 percent of carbon stored in the world's tropical forests is contained within Indigenous territories and that Indigenous groups are the most effective stewards of these important carbon sinks, especially when provided with land titles and adequate resources.[80]

Indigenous activists would also organise powerful interventions and protests in the streets (and rivers) of Paris. Indigenous representatives from North and South America, Indonesia and Congo were part of a flotilla of 'kayaktivists' on the Seine, paddling with a ceremonial 'Canoe of Life' that had been brought from the Ecuadorian Amazon.[81] During the COP21 Solutions Concert, they took over the stage led by the 17 year old US indigenous activist and rapper Xiuhtezcatl Tonatiuh, an action which was shut down by event organizers. At the end of COP21, on December 12th (abbreviated to D12), indigenous nations of the Circumpolar, Amazon, South Pacific and North America joined for an early morning sunrise ceremony at the foot of the historic Notre Dame Cathedral. The ceremony was disrupted by police who descended upon the square and began to rudely remove banners during the prayer. Participants then occupied the Pont des Arts bridge, famous for its love padlocks, and spread enormous red banners across the span of River Seine symbolising that indigenous people are the 'Red Line' against the privatisation of nature, dirty fossil fuels and climate change.[82]

On the Streets

The rest of D12 would see two enormous mass demonstrations denouncing the inadequate outcome of COP21 and serving to remind the State leaders of the strength and persistence of grassroots citizen movements. In light of the ongoing state of emergency in France, where public demonstrations were banned, both were held in defiance of such authoritarian law, though they were eventually authorised by the City of Paris and instead guarded by a tight security presence, including mandatory 'pat down' searches. First, a demonstration was held beneath the Arc-du-Triomphe along l'avenue de la Grande Armée which leads to the financial district, La Défense. The avenue was blocked in an act of civil disobedience aimed at denouncing the role of finance and corporate capitalism in the climate crisis, much in the vein of 'Flood Wall Street' after the People's Climate March in New York City just over a year previously. The action was well prepared for, with several training workshops in civil disobedience organised at the Climate Action Zone. However, so numerous and civil were the thousands of participants that it was a very calm and peaceful protest. Massive red banners were unfurled symbolising the red lines of no-compromise on climate justice. To commemorate the victims of climate change, the crowd wore red, paused for a minute's silence at 12pm on the 12th day of the 12th month and then distributed flowers. The crowds at the demonstration exploded into festivity, marching bands wandered joyously singing old anarchist songs and there was much art and creativity of banners, placards and costumes.

The demonstration in Champ-de-Mars, in the shadow of the Eiffel Tower, would be the climactic, and final, grassroots demonstration at COP21. Declaring "a state of emergency for the climate, " they denounced as catastrophic the estimated +3 °C warming based on countries' total INDC commitments under the Paris Agreement. This demonstration consisted of an enormous human chain, three lines thick, along both lengths of the Champ-de-Mars as a visual act of solidarity and hope. There were also flash mobs, several keynote speeches and finally a concert to end on a high note. Such a demonstration ensured that the movements would have the last word regarding COP 21.

Elsewhere and at other times throughout the city, novel forms of demonstrating without breaking the law were dreamed up: a giant geo-localisation activity that saw demonstrators arrange themselves, scattered throughout the streets of Paris, to form the words 'Climate, Justice, Peace' which displayed on a geo-localisation map on the website of Greenpeace France. Similar innovation was struck up in the week preceding COP21 in a poignant demonstration of thousands of pairs of shoes silently arranged in rows in lieu of human protesters in la Place de la République. On another day, an artists' demonstration was held outside of the Louvre, protesting the role of fossil fuel companies in the cultural world. The Louvre, the most exceptional art museum in France and possibly the world, includes Eni and Total, two European oil and gas companies, amongst its sponsors. Defying a thick police presence, the artists brandished black umbrellas which, once opened, they used to make a wall reading "Fossil Free Culture". They were accompanied by breathtaking 'Climate Guardians' from Australia, white angels gracefully hovering on stilts stunning onlookers for their other wordlly tranquility.

It Takes Roots to Weather the Storm

These five streams represented very different aspects of COP21: the Blue Zone negotiation rooms; the Green Zone exhibits; the summit of mayors; the Montreuil festival; and the Climate Action Zone and associated protest actions in the streets. However, to what extent these five streams overlap or converge is not so evident. One thing is certain, the climate movement is becoming radicalised, slowly but surely. At the Alternatiba Festival in Montreuil and the Climate Action Zone, civil disobedience was being planned for the next few months through occupations of mines, fossil fuel installations, petroleum carrying railways and so on. A boycott was also being called for to encourage the withdrawal of investment funding in polluting industries.

The dominant politico-economic system is likely to be put under pressure by much of the 99%. But if the history of past protest movements is indicative, there will come a point when today's movements have to plant deeper roots in the neighbourhoods and cities and attract many more thousands of concerned citizens. Meanwhile the power elite will continue to declare good intentions and sign this or that treaty, symbolic actions which may momentarily distract some. The science of climate change, however, and its forecasts cannot be ignored. Sooner or later, the movement advocating systemic change has to engage in the radical perspective of structural change of the major politico-economic institutions and proceed in democratising democracy.

Given the evident resistance to changes by nation-states, their multi-national bodies and the 400 dominant corporations driving the world economy that influence them, what are the levers to transform this situation? In a global context where the dominant paradigm can be increasingly summed up by the equation 'happiness = consumption', people need to be empowered and to become engaged citizens by obtaining the means to access alternatives that can make a difference and open up horizons for a better quality of life.

Beyond all the false solutions based on the premise that technology, the capitalist market and its financial mechanisms will somehow naturally protect the planet from climate change, there exist some real alternatives. A number of local governments are already experimenting with new systems of production and consumption and are promoting sustainable alternatives. In a number of sectors including that of agriculture, energy, waste management, transportation and construction, citizens all over the world are conceiving and fueling initiatives that are playing a part in reducing greenhouse gas emissions and improving people's quality of life.

The current actions taking place are living proof that, all over the world, whether at the local, regional or global level, women and men are taking action, driven by the desire and the need to build societies that are fair and more respectful of the planet's limits. The success of these initiatives helps to shift the balance of power. As this thrust meets the inevitable resistance of both State and Capital, it will need to deepen its revolutionary vision, and will have to move on a road map which seeks to abolish all exploitation and domination as such.

Changing the social relations of our society is basic to movement building, which requires the realisation of fundamental equality between women and men, between young and old, and between all citizens and nationalities. Of the various forms of political ecology, only social ecology as advanced by thinkers like Murray Bookchin, and developed and argued by others since his death in 2006, can help us draw a road map outlining the fundamental transformation needed. The massive rural-urban migration taking place now, with its concomitant deformed urbanisation as a consequence, is forcing a serious questioning about the kind of cities that we want. However, we can only radically evolve toward ecological and democratic cities by using the lens of social ecology which takes us beyond the narrowness of environmentalism. Moreover, the old Left socialist solutions of the State ownership of this or that part of the economy will only take us back to those old dilemmas from which we have worked hard to free ourselves. Social ecologists insist that the environmental or ecological crisis is not a crisis in Nature but a social crisis centered on our type of society and which, thus, requires a total transformation of our society, root and branch.

Notes - Preface 2019

1. Chris Cillizza and Sam Petulla, "Trump is on pace to sign more executive orders than any president in the last 50 years," *CNN Politics*, October 13, 2017. https://cnn.it/2POO1U3
2. Tess Riley, "Just 100 companies responsible for 71% of global emissions, study says," *The Guardian,* July 10, 2017. https://bit.ly/2t4jSo2
3. Nadja Popovich, Livia Albeck Ripka, and Kendra Pierre Louis, "76 Environmental Rules on the Way Out Under Trump," *The New York Times,* July 6, 2018. https://nyti.ms/2hPvpI8; David Cutler, and Francesca Dominici, "JAMA Forum: A Breath of Bad Air: Trump Environmental Agenda May Lead to 80000 Extra Deaths per Decade." *JAMA,* May 10, 2018. https://bit.ly/2KTm37R
4. Ibid. https://nyti.ms/2hPvpI8; https://bit.ly/2KTm37R.
5. Richard Rorty, *Achieving Our Country* (Cambridge, Harvard University Press: 1998).
6. Gary Langer, "Nearly half of Americans think there's a 'deep state': Poll," *ABC News*, Apr 27, 2017. https://abcn.ws/2QDD0de "Public Troubled by 'Deep State,'" *Monmouth University website,* March 19, 2018. https://bit.ly/2pvHOlF
7. "The Latest: Clinton has twice as many six-figure donors," *U.S. News: A World Report,* October 15, 2016. https://bit.ly/2QFUK7V; Patrick Morris, "President Obama Spent $684 Million to Get Elected. You'll Never Guess How Much Wall Street Chipped In," *The Motley Fool,* December 28, 2013. https://bit.ly/2EvK2cN. Kristin Jensen and Christine Harper, "Obama Top Fundraiser on Wall Street," *Bloomberg News,* April 18, 2007. https://wapo.st/2A3WtJW In 2012, Obama even raised double

what his Republican opponent Mitt Romney raised from Bain Capital, a Boston-based private-equity firm Romney himself co-founded. (Source: Dan Eggen and T.W. Farnam, "Obama still flush with cash from financial sector despite frosty relations," *The Washington Post*, October 19, 2011. https://wapo.st/2A3WtJW)

8. Miles Kampf-Lassin, "Centrism Is in a Death Spiral: Our Only Hope Is to Let It Perish," *In These Times*, July 9, 2017. https://bit.ly/2ut2jCB; Sean Keady, "If the Future of the Democratic Party Means Winning Elections, Count Me Out," *McSweeney's*, January 16, 2019. https://bit.ly/2Fni2qx

9. Edward-Isaac Dovere, "Bernie's army in disarray," *Politico,* May 21, 2018. https://politi.co/2IPUq1R

10. Jonathan Watts, "We have 12 years to limit climate change catastrophe, warns UN," *The Guardian,* October 8, 2018. https://bit.ly/2E7MhED. IPCC Secretariat, *Summary for Policymakers of IPCC Special Report on Global Warming of 1.5°C approved by governments*, October 8, 2018. https://bit.ly/2A5BEhi

11. Fourth National Climate Assessment. Volume II: Impacts, Risks, and Adaptation in the United States. 23 November 2018. https://nca2018.globalchange.gov

12. "WMO Provisional statement on the State of the Global Climate in 2018," *World Meteorological Organization,* November 26, 2018. https://bit.ly/2PYRgNz; Michael Irving, "State of the Climate report paints 2018 as a devastating, record-breaking year," *New Atlas,* November 30, 2018. https://bit.ly/2Gx5qRP

13. Eve Andrews, "How did the environment do on the 2018 ballot?", *The Grist*, November 7, 2018. https://bit.ly/2RF1vmp

14. Naomi Klein, "The Game-Changing Promise of a Green New Deal," *The Intercept,* November 28, 2018. https://bit.ly/2zwqAtb

15. Paul Potter's Speech in Washington DC, April 17, 1965, *Rebels With a Cause* website. http://www.sdsrebels.com/potter.htm
16. Bertrand Russell, "Civil Disobedience," *New Statesman*, February 17, 1961.
17. Mario Savio, Speech on the steps of Sproul Hall, December 2, 1964. https://en.wikiquote.org/wiki/Mario_Savio
18. Martin Luther King Jr., *Letter from a Birmingham Jail*, April 16, 1963. http://www.africa.upenn.edu/Articles_Gen/Letter_Birmingham.html
19. Joshua Hawley and Dimitrios Roussopoulos (eds.), *Villages in Cities: Community Land Ownership, Cooperative Housing, and the Milton Parc Story,* (Montreal: Black Rose Books, 2019). https://bit.ly/2TOZUAf
20. Benjamin Barber in Richard Florida, "If Cities Ruled the World," *CityLab,* April 26, 2017. https://bit.ly/2EDBmlI
21. Ibid.
22. See Murray Bookchin, *Urbanization without Cities*, (Montreal: Black Rose Books, 1992).

Notes

1. See Peter A. Kropotkin, *Fields, Factories and Workshops*, first published in 1899; republished with an introduction by George Woodcock (Montreal: Black Rose Books, 1994).
2. Isidore Geoffroy-Saint-Hilaire, *Histoire naturelle des règnes organiques*, Volume II (Paris: Masson, 1859).
3. Ernest Haeckel, "Über Entwickelungsgang und Aufgabe der Zoologie," *Jenaische Zeitschrift*, 5 (1870).
4. Donald Worster, *Nature's Economy* (San Francisco: Sierra Club Books, 1977), 67.
5. Great Plains Committee, *The Future of the Great Plains* (Washington, DC: US Government Printing Office, 1936).
6. See Holly Sklar (ed.), *Trilateralism: The Trilateral Commission and Elite Planning for World Management* (Montreal: Black Rose Books, 1980).
7. Council on Environmental Quality, "Environmental Quality 1970" (Washington, DC: US Government Printing Office, 1970), 38.
8. Jean Mary Haley (ed.), *Open Options: A Guide to Stockholm's Alternative Environmental Conferences* (Stockholm, 1972).
9. Michael Clow, "Ecological Exhaustion and the Global Crisis of Capitalism," *Our Generation*, 23: 1 (1992).
10. See *Les traités alternatif de Rio* (Montreal: Editions Ecosociété, 1994).
11. Wolfgang Burhenne (ed.), *International Environmental Law: Multilateral Treaties* (Berlin: E. Schmidt Verlag, 1985).
12. Ronald B. Mitchell, 2002-2017. *International Environmental Agreements Database Project* (Version 2017.1). Available at http://iea.uoregon.edu/.
13. Al Gore, *Earth in the Balance* (New York: Plume/Penguin, 1993), 82.

14. ibid., 73.
15. ibid., 156.
16. ibid., 10.
17. Philip Lowe and Jane Gayder, *Environmental Groups in Politics* (London: George Allen & Unwin, 1983), 1.
18. ibid.
19. Council on Environmental Quality, "Environmental Quality 1980" (Washington, DC: US Government Printing office, 1980), 418-422.
20. Michael Tobias (ed.), *Deep Ecology* (San Marcos: Avant Books, 1984).
21. Judith Plant, "Searching for Common Ground: Ecofeminism and Bioregionalism," in Irene Diamond and Gloria Feman Orenstein (eds.), *Reweaving the World* (San Francisco: Sierra Book Club, 1991), 158.
22. Kirkpatrick Sale, "Bioregionalism," in Andrew Dobson (ed.), *The Green Reader* (London: Andre Deutsch, 1991), 79.
23. "Towards a New Politics: Principles and Program of the Vermont and New Hampshire Greens," *Our Generation*, 20: 1 (1988), 22-54.
24. Carolyn Merchant, *Radical Ecology* (New York: Routledge, 1992).
25. Janet Biehl, *Finding Our Way: Rethinking Ecofeminist Politics* (Montreal: Black Rose Books, 1991).
26. Biehl quoted in Merchant, *Radical Ecology*, 195.
27. Öcalan, Abdullah, *Democratic Confederalism* (Cologne: International Initiative, 2011) and Öcalan, Abdullah, *Liberating Life: Woman's Revolution* (Cologne: International Initiative, 2013).
28. Andrew Dobson, *Green Political Thought* (London: Unwin Hyman, 1990), 13.

29. Jonathan Porritt, *Seeing Green: The Politics of Ecology Explained* (Oxford: Blackwell, 1984), 87-88.
30. ibid., 87.
31. James O'Connor, "Socialism and Ecology," *Our Generation*, 22: 1&2, (1990-91), 81.
32. Penny Kemp, *Europe's Green Alternative: Manifesto for a New World* (Montreal: Black Rose Books, 1992).
33. ibid., 41.
34. ibid., 42-43.
35. ibid., 62.
36. ibid., 94.
37. Murray Bookchin, "Postscript: Ecologizing the Dialectic," in John P. Clark (ed.), *Renewing the Earth: The Promise of Social Ecology* (London: Green Print, 1990), 202; emphasis in original.
38. Murray Bookchin, "The Meaning of Confederalism," *Our Generation*, 22: 1&2 (1990-91), 98.
39. ibid., 99.
40. ibid., 95.
41. ibid., 95-96.
42. David Harvey, "The Urban Roots of Capitalist Crisis," in *Rebel Cities: From the Right to the City to the Urban Revolution* (London: Verso, 2012), 27-28.
43. ibid.
44. Robert Park, *On Social Control and Collective Behavior* (Chicago: University of Chicago Press, 1976), 3.
45. Elif Genc, "Meet the Women of the HDP: Gender, Resistance and Radical Democracy," *The Bullet: The Socialist Project*, E-Bulletin, 1133 (June 24, 2015).
46. Abdullah Öcalan, *Democratic Confederalism* (Cologne: International Initiative, 2011).

47. David Harvey, "The Right to the City," *New Left Review*, 53 (1998), 23.
48. Social Forum of the Americas and World Urban Forum, *The World Charter for the Right to the City* (2004; available at urbanreinventors.net).
49. United Cities and Local Governments: Committee on Social Inclusion, Participatory Democracy and Human Rights, *The Global Charter: Agenda for Human Rights in the City* (2012; available at uclg-cisdp.org).
50. The European based Transnational Institute of Social Ecology (TRISE) continually discusses such a strategy with a view to its implementation.
51. Graham Turner and Cathy Alexander, "'Limits of Growth' was right: New research shows we're nearing collapse," *The Guardian*, September 2, 2014.
52. Nafeez Ahmed, "Scientific model supported by UK Government Taskforce flags risk of civilisation's collapse by 2040," *Insurge Intelligence*, June 19, 2015 (available at medium.com).
53. Sophia Ruess and Jennifer Geleff, "Three Minutes to Midnight: Natural Catastrophes in the Anthropocene," in *Alternatives International Journal*, July 1, 2015.
54. Rob Jordan, "Stanford researcher declares that the sixth mass extinction is here," *Stanford Report*, June 19, 2015.
55. Sophia Ruess, "Lampedusa: European Border Delocalization in the Mediterranean," *Alternatives International Journal*, June 2015.
56. Global Sustainability Institute, *Food, Climate Change and War: The Syria Crisis*, Anglia Ruskin University News, September 2013.
57. Gustave Massiah, *The Strategy for the Alternative to Globalisation* (Montreal: Black Rose Books, 2015).

58. For more information on the INDCs and estimates of their consequences, see the 'Climate Action Tracker': http://climateactiontracker.org/
59. Bill McKibben, "Falling Short on Climate in Paris," *New York Times*, December 13, 2015. https://www.nytimes.com/2015/12/14/opinion/falling-short-on-climate-in-paris.html?_r=0
60. Directorate General for Internal Policies, "Emission Reduction Targets for Aviation and Shipping", *Policy Department A: Economic and Scientific Policy of the European Parliament*, November 2015. Retrieved at: http://www.europarl.europa.eu/RegData/etudes/STUD/2015/569964/IPOL_STU(2015)569964_EN.pdf
61. Mitch Paquette, "Indigenous Rights Cut from Paris Agreement: Why it Concerns Us All," *Intercontinental Cry*, January 13, 2016. Retrieved at: https://intercontinentalcry.org/indigenous-rights-cut-from-paris-agreement-why-it-concerns-us-all/
62. John Vidal, "How a 'typo' nearly derailed the Paris climate deal," *The Guardian*, December 16, 2015.
63. Doyle Rice, "175 nations sign historic Paris climate deal on Earth Day," *The USA TODAY*, April 22, 2016. https://www.usatoday.com/story/news/world/2016/04/22/paris-climate-agreement-signing-united-nations-new-york/83381218/4
64. Peter H. Gleick, "Water, Drought, Climate Change, and Conflict in Syria," *American Meteorological Society*, 6 (2014): 331-340.
65. "Global Land and Ocean Temperature Anomalies in Degrees Celsius, Jan 1980-June 2016 vs. Base Period 1901-2000," NOAA's National Centers for Environmental Information.
66. Christophe Bonneuil, "Tous responsables ?" *Le Monde diplomatique*, (Novembre 2015). For more on the 'Capitalocene', see Jason Moore, *Capitalism in the Web of Life: Ecology and the*

Accumulation of Capital, (London: Verso, 2015) and Andreas Malm, *Fossil Capital: The Rise of Steam-Power and the Roots of Global Warming*, (London: Verso, 2015).

67. ibid.
68. A useful source on the history of the corporate capture of UN climate conferences is Pascoe Sabido, *The Corporate Cookbook: How Climate Criminals Have Captured COP21*, (Brussels: Corporate Europe Observatory, 2015). See: http://corporateeurope.org/climate-and-energy/2015/11/corporate-cookbook.
69. Corporate Europe Observatory, *Lobby Planet Paris – A Guide to Corporate COP 21*, November 2015. Retrieved from: http://corporateeurope.org/sites/default/files/attachments/lobbyguide_en_small.pdf
70. Pascoe Sabido, *The Corporate Cookbook: How Climate Criminals have Captured COP21.*
71. ibid., 6.
72. Source of diagram: *Lobby Planet Paris – A Guide to Corporate COP 21,* November 2015. Retrieved from: http://corporateeurope.org/sites/default/files/attachments/lobbyguide_en_small.pdf
73. Pascoe Sabido, *The Corporate Cookbook: How Climate Criminals have Captured COP21.*
74. Lindsay Abrams, "Exxon CEO ridicules green energy: 'We choose not to lose money on purpose,'" *Salon,* May 28, 2015. http://www.salon.com/2015/05/28/exxon_ceo_ridicules_green_energy_we_choose_not_to_lose_money_on_purpose/
75. ibid.
76. "COP21: Eco activists Brandalism launch Paris ad takeover," *BBC News,* November 29, 2015. Retrieved at: http://www.bbc.com/news/world-europe-34958282

Political Ecology

77. Rachel Tansey, *Dirty Hands on Dirty Deals: TTIP and COP21 Shaped by same Big Business Interests.* Corporate Europe Observatory, November 2015. Retrieved from: https://corporateeurope.org/sites/default/files/dirtydeals_small.pdf
78. The full four hour-long round table discussion, "From COP21 to Habitat III: local governments and citizens at the heart of the challenges", organised by the UCLG CISDP, was recorded and is available here: https://www.youtube.com/watch?v=UngeD_g6-lA
79. For more information on the Global Platform for the Right to the City, see: http://www.righttothecityplatform.org.br/
80. Mike Gaworecki, "Indigenous leaders at COP21: 20 per cent of tropical forest carbon is sitting on indigenous land," *Eco-Business*, December 3, 2015. Retrieved at: http://www.eco-business.com/news/indigenous-leaders-at-cop21-20-per-cent-of-tropical-forest-carbon-is-sitting-on-indigenous-land/
81. Martin Lukacs, "Indigenous activists take to Seine river to protest axing of rights from Paris climate pact," *The Guardian,* December 7, 2015.
82. "Press release: Indigenous Peoples Take Lead at D12 Day of Action in Paris – Official response to COP21 agreement." December 12, 2015. Retrieved from: http://indigenousrising.org/indigenous-peoples-take-lead-at-d12-day-of-action-in-paris-official-response-to-cop21-agreement/

Bibliography

Abélès, Marc, *Le Defi Ecologiste* (Paris: L'Harmattan, 1993).

Aldous, Tony, *Battle for the Environment* (London: Fontana, 1972).

Allan Michaud, Dominique, *L'avenir de la société alternative* (Paris: L'Harmattan, 1989).

Alphandery, Pierre and Pierre Bitoun, Yves Dupont, *L'équivoque écologique* (Paris: La Découverte, 1991).

Barkun, Michael, *Disaster and the Millenium* (New Haven: Yale University Press, 1974).

Bennahmias, Jean-Luc and Agnès Roche, *Des verts de toutes les couleurs* (Paris: Albin Michel, 1992).

Boardman, Robert, *International Organization and the Conservation of Nature* (Bloomington: Indiana University Press, 1981).

Bookchin, Murray, *Toward an Ecological Society (*Montreal: Black Rose Books, 1981).

—— *The Philosophy of Social Ecology*, revised edition *(*Montreal: Black Rose Books, 1995).

Bowman, James S., "The Ecology Movement: A Viewpoint," *International journal of Environmental Studies,* 8:2 (1975): 91-97.

Bowman, James S., "The Environmental Movement: An Assessment of Ecological Politics," *Environmental Affairs,* 5:4 (1976): 649-667.

Boy, Daniel. L'écologisme en France: évolution et structures" (Atelier: L'Écologisme politique, constances et différences au niveau européen), Paris: *European Consortium for Political Research,* Fondation Nationales des Sciences Politiques, 10-15 April 1989.

Cans, Roger, *Tous Verts* (Paris: Calmann-Levy, 1992).

Chafe, Tony, "The Greens and the municipal election," *Association for the Study of Modern and Contemporary France,* 14 (May-June, 1983).

Clarke, Robin, and Lloyd Timberlake, *Stockholm Plus Ten* (London: Earthscan, 1982).

Cotgrove, Stephen, *Catastrophe or Cornucopia: The Environment, Politics and Future* (Chichester: John Wiley & Sons, 1982).

Dasmann, Raymond F, J.P. Milton, and P.H. Freeman, *Ecologicial Principles for Economic Development* (London: John Wiley, 1973).

Day, Alan J., and Henry W. Degenhart, *Political Parties of the World* (Detroit: Gale Research Co., 1984).

Doud, Alden L., "International Environmental Developments: Perceptions of Developing and Developed Countries," *Natural Resources Journal, 12* (October 1972): 520-529.

Dumont, Rene, *L'Utopie ou la mort (*Paris: Seuil, 1973).

Enzensberger, Hans Magnus, "A Critique of Political Ecology," *New Left Review, 84* (March-April 1974): 3-31.

Fox, Stephen, *John Muir and His Legacy: The American Conservation Movement (*Boston: Little, Brown & Co., 1981).

Golub, Robert and Jo Townsend, "Malthus, Multinationals and the Club of Rome," *Social Studies of Science, 7* (1977): 201-222.

Haley, Mary Jean (ed.), *Open Options: A Guide to Stockholm's Alternative Environmental Conferences,* Stockholm: 29 May 1972.

Hardin, Charles M., "Observations on Environmental Politics," in Stuart S. Nagel (ed.), *Environmental Politics* (London: Prager, 1974).

Harvey, David, "The Right to the City," *New Left Review,* 53 (1998).

—— "The Urban Roots of Capitalist Crisis," *Rebel Cities: From the Right to the City to the Urban Revolution* (London: Verso, 2012).

Huth, Hans, *Nature and the American: Three Centuries of Changing Attitudes* (Berkeley: University of California Press, 1957).

Johnson, Stanley. *The Politics of Environment: The British Experience* (London: Tom Stacey, 1973).

Kemp, Penny, *Europe's Green Alternative: Manifesto for a New World* (Montreal: Black Rose Books, 1992).

Kropotkin, Peter, *Fields, Factories and Workshops* (Montreal: Black Rose Books, 1993).

Massiah, Gustave, *The Strategy for the Alternative to Globalisation* (Montreal: Black Rose Books, 2015).

Mayer, Sylvie, *Parti pris pour l'écologie* (Paris: Messidor/Editions Sociales, 1990).

Milbrath, Lester W., *Environmentalists: Vanguard for a New Society* (New York: State University of N.Y. Press in Albany, 1984).

Morgan, Robin, and Brian Whitaker, *Rainbow Warrior* (London: Arrow Books, 1986).

National Academy of Sciences, *International Arrangements of International Environmental Co-operation* (Washington, DC: NAS, 1972).

National Parks Service, *First World Conference on National Parks* (Washington DC: Department of the Interior, 1962).

Öcalan, Abdullah, *Democratic Confederalism* (Cologne: International Initiative, 2011).

Ophuls, William, *Ecology and the Politics of Scarcity* (San Francisco: W.H. Freeman, 1977).

Organisation for Economic Cooperation and Development, *The OECD Program on Long Range Transport of Air Pollutants*, Summary Report (Paris: OECD, 1977).

—— *The State of the Environment, 1979* (Paris: OECD, 1979).

—— *The State of the Environment, 1985* (Paris: OECD, 1985).

O'Riordan, Timothy, *Environmentalism* (London: Pion, 1981).

Papadakis, Elim, "The Green Party in Contemporary West German Politics," *Political Quarterly*, 54:2 (July-September 1983).

Penick, James. *Progressive Politics and Conservation* (Chicago: University of Chicago Press, 1968).

Petulla, J. M., *American Environmentalism: Values, Tactics, Priorities* (College Station: Texas A&M University Press, 1980).

Porritt, Jonathan, *Seeing Green: The Politics of Ecology Explained* (Oxford: Blackwell, 1984).

Pursell, Carroll (ed.), *From Conservation to Ecology: The Development Concern* (New York: Thomas Y. Crowell Co., 1973).

Ridgeway, James, *The Politics of Ecology* (New York: E.P. Dutton, 1970).

Rosenbaum, Walter, *Environmental Politics and Policy* (Washington, D.C.: CQ Press, 1985).

Sandbach, Francis, "The Rise and Fall of the Limits of Growth Debate," *Social Studies of Science,* 8:4 (November 1978): 495-520.

Sainteny, Guillaume, *Les Verts* (Paris: P.U.F, 1991).

Schnaiberg, Allen, "Politics, Participation and Pollution: The Environmental Movement," in John Walton and Donald E. Carns (eds.), *Cities in Change: Studies in the Urban Condition* (Boston: Allen and Bacon Inc., 1977).

Simonnet, Dominique, *L'écologisme* (Paris: P.U.F, 1979).

Stone, Peter, *Did We Save The Planet at Stockholm?* (London: Earth Island, 1973).

Touraine, Alain, *La prophétie anti-nucléaire* (Paris: Seuil, 1980).

―― *The Voice and the Eye: An Analysis of Social Movements* (Cambridge: Cambridge University Press, 1980).

Tozzi, Michel, *Syndicalism et nouveaux mouvements sociaux: Régionalisme, féminisme et écologie* (Lyon: Ed. Ouvrières,1982).

United Cities and Local Governments: Committee on Social Inclusion, Participatory Democracy and Human Rights, *The Global Charter: Agenda for Human Rights in the City,* 2012.

United Nations Environmental Program, *Report of the Governing Council of the UNEP, Fourth Session, 1976* (Nairobi: UNEP, 1976).

―― *Register of International Treaties and Other Agreements in the Field of the Environment* (Nairobi: UNEP, 1984).